INSIGHT COMPACT GUIDES

SYDNEY

D0418230

Compact Guide: Sydney is the ideal quick-reference guide to Australia's pre-eminent city. It tells you all you need to know about Sydney's attractions, from the Opera House to the Harbour Bridge and from the Botanic Gradens to Bondi Beach.

This is one of more than 90 titles in *Apa Publications'* new series of pocket-sized, easy-to-use guidebooks intended for the independent-minded traveller. *Compact Guides* are in essence travel encyclopedias in miniature, designed to be comprehensive yet portable, as well as up-to-date and authoritative.

Star Attractions

An instant reference to some of Sydney's top attractions to help you set your priorities.

Sydney Harbour Bridge p17

Opera House p18

Royal Botanic Gardens p19

The Rocks p22

Monorail p29

National Maritime Museum p31

Oxford Street p36

Bondi p39

Taronga Zoo p54

Chinatown p33

Shelley Beach p57

Sydney

Introduction

Places

Culture

Leisure

Practical Information

Sydney – Capital of the Pacific Rim

Opposite: Bondi babe

Sydney Harbour with its racing yachts, the lifesavers at Bondi Beach, the pearly white sails of the Opera House… to the exasperation of Australia's other cities, most of the symbols that define the country to the outside world are located in one glittering corner of its east coast. Almost all international flights arrive in Sydney, and many foreign visitors see no good reason to leave. Here, in one of the world's youngest cities, Australia's easygoing hedonism finds its most spectacular backdrop, and leisure has been elevated to an art form.

At this once-remote fringe of the globe, cultural and natural attractions effortlessly mingle. Sydney is more integrated with the sea than Rio or Honolulu: there are no fewer than 70 beaches within the city boundaries, and the magnificent harbour runs through its heart (the green and yellow harbour ferries are perhaps the world's most pleasant form of commuter transport, and should be taken whenever possible). Dramatic sandstone bluffs line the city's borders; great stretches of pristine bushland are part of its urban fabric. Yet, with 4 million inhabitants, Sydney is also an unstoppable cultural centre, with a thriving art scene, booming film industry, myriad museums, galleries and theatres, a round-the-clock nightlife and some of the finest (and most dramatically-located) restaurants on earth. No wonder that the city has become a symbol of the booming Pacific in recent years: when the Olympics committee had to decide where to hold the games in the year 2000, Sydney was the obvious choice.

Taking it easy

5

Dramatic vistas

Such prominence does arouse some envy. To its critics – who mostly seem to live in Australia's traditional rival city, Melbourne, or the official capital, Canberra – Sydney is all glitz, obsessed with superficial show, flash money, appearances above substance. Urban planners also carp: in recent years, the city's urban sprawl has become enormous (the city's area, in fact, is twice as large as Beijing's, with mile after mile of orange-roofed suburbia). But none of this seems to matter to most Sydneysiders, and even less to visitors. The city is continually being 'Manhattanised' – luring the wealthiest, smartest and most artistically talented from the rest of Australia, while real estate values go through the roof.

The capital of New South Wales, Sydney is the oldest and largest city in Australia, and while there are other great Australian cities, Sydney is the country's only *world* city: Sydneysiders compare their achievements not with Melbourne, Brisbane or Canberra, but New York, London and Paris. Increasingly, in recent years, Sydney has become

less a Western city oddly placed in the Antipodes – as it was regarded for much of its history – but a booming nexus of South-East Asia, with massive Asian migration and a vast array of resident millionaires. It's a strange fate for a city that was founded, in 1788, as a dumping ground for British prisoners. These days, everybody wants to live in 'the capital of the Pacific Rim' – or the 'Best Address on Earth', as Sydneysiders humbly think of their home.

From rags to riches

The convict past

Indeed, few of the world's great cities have had so wretched a start. In the 1780s, after the American War of Independence, the British government could no longer look across the Atlantic for a place to expel its growing number of convicts. The prison hulks of the Thames were soon filled to overflowing with pickpockets and petty vagabonds, who had mostly been caught stealing loaves of bread or a handful of grain to survive. Finally, the naturalist Sir Joseph Banks came up with an extraordinary plan: the dregs of British society could be transported to the other end of the earth and deposited in the Antipodes, which Banks had visited on his journey with Captain James Cook some years earlier. It would be a nine month voyage, covering 15,000km; nothing quite like it had been attempted in history before.

On 26 January 1788, a fleet of 11 ships under the command of Captain Arthur Phillip sailed into Sydney harbour (which they named after Lord Sydney, the London Home Secretary, rejecting the Arthurian 'Albion'). They landed a sea-sick gaggle of male convicts and their military jailers – an unsavoury group of naval recruits well schooled in rum, sodomy and the lash – while the local Eora Aborigines let out furious howls and threw stones to drive them away. The officers pitched their tents east of the fresh-water Tank Stream at Sydney Cove, the prisoners and their guards to the west (creating a social division that lasts to this day, with the wealthier suburbs of the east versus the less affluent of the west). Two weeks later, the women convicts disembarked with the many children that had been born on the voyage. An extra rum ration was handed out, a violent storm began, and the 736 felons of the young colony – along with not a few of their randy guards – descended into a drunken orgy.

Convict heritage in Hyde Park Barracks

This unlikely settlement at Sydney Cove faced near-starvation for the next decade, but clung on precariously to the fringe of this eerie, inhospitable land, where the seasons were back-to-front and exotic animals hopped instead of ran. More convicts arrived, followed by the first free British settlers, turning Sydney into the beach-head for the conquest of the Australian continent. And the claiming of Sydney set the pattern for the country's future: the en-

tire continent was simply declared a *terra nullius*, or no-man's land (nomadic aboriginals, it was decided, simply did not use or possess homes), and a new colony was born.

Sydneysiders take their recreation seriously

Multi-cultural society

7

Looking around Sydney today, it's hard to believe that as recently as 1939, a survey showed that Sydney's population was 98 percent of Anglo-Celtic stock, and local newspapers were proudly proclaiming that Australia was the most 'British' country on earth. In this monochromatic society, the only unusual accents were of the 'new chums' from corners of Ireland or the Scottish highlands; foods were rarely more exotic than Yorkshire pudding; Christmas was a time for huge Dickensian meals of roast beef or pork, no matter how brutally tropical the weather.

The multicultural mix

All that changed after 1945, when Australia embarked on one of the most ambitious immigration programmes of the modern era, and Sydney was the first port of call. The first migrants mostly came from Greece, Italy and Eastern Europe; in the 1970s, the century-old 'White Australia' policy was finally abandoned, and new Aussies arrived from every corner of the globe. Statistics only begin to tell the story: in the past 50 years, more than 1.5 million settlers from 200 countries have made Sydney their home. Today, four out of 10 Sydneysiders are migrants or their first-generation children; half of them come from non-English speaking backgrounds. More than 40 percent of settler arrivals now come from Asia, while British and Irish make up only 18 percent.

The post-war influx has radically changed the structure and habits of Sydney society. Take a seat on the Manly ferry today and you're just as likely to be sitting next to the daughter of a builder harking from Athens, a journalist from Naples, a car salesman from Thailand or a doctor from Lebanon. And the guiding principle of Australia's

Chinatown dining

immigration policy, and society in general, has become 'multi-culturalism' – tolerance and respect for all cultures and races.

Even so, immigrant groups have congregated in their own distinctive areas; for a visitor, this can most easily be seen through the city's restaurants. Sydney's 'Little Italy' is the suburb of Leichardt, where some of the best pasta outside Rome can be had; Chinatown is around Dixon Street in the inner city; to the west, Cabramatta feels like a slice of old Saigon. Greeks tend to congregate around Marrickville, Koreans in Campsie, Turks in Auburn, and South Americans in Newtown and Fairfield.

The Sydney spirit

Office workers

Looking on a map, many visitors still think of Sydney as a gateway to the vast deserts of Australia; there is a persistent vision of the 'true Aussie' as a sun-bronzed stockman or jillaroo, riding the rural range with trusty sheep dog, fiercely independent, in love with land, wind, dust and sun. Of course, nothing could be further from day-to-day reality. Australia is the most urbanised country on earth, and Sydney, like all its large cities, remains relentlessly clinging to the coast, obsessed with the beach. Meanwhile, the 'true Aussie' is now a Sydney office worker, living ensconced on his or her plot of land in suburbia, with a brick house, red tile roof, Hill's Hoist washing line, 1.5 children and barbie in the backyard.

Most Sydneysiders wouldn't recognise a trough of sheep dip if they fell in it. And although many suburbanites still see the Outback as somehow embodying the most distinctive part of the country – and may even get about at times in a bushie's hat adorned with croc teeth, or the 'Driza-bone' raincoat – relatively few have visited it, let alone considered living there. Even Patrick White, who set famous novels like *Voss* in the furthest red-sand-and-spinifex deserts, never actually saw them (he got his images from his friend Sidney Nolan's paintings). White settled in the Eastern Suburbs of Sydney, a stone's throw, relatively speaking, from the water.

This doesn't mean that the key element of the Aussie image isn't true: Sydneysiders are perhaps the most outdoor-loving people on earth. The only thing is that they love to be surrounded by beach sand, not desert.

Cliffs at The Gap

'How shall I put this delicately?' asks Sydney writer Robert Drewe (who himself lives in Sydney's Elizabeth Bay, gazing at the harbour). 'Most Australians of the past three generations have had their first sexual experience on the coast. So is it surprising that for the rest of their lives the sexual and littoral experience are entwined in their memories; that most Australians thereafter see the beach in a pleasurable light?' It is to the sea that Australians return at each crucial stage of their lives: as lovers, on honeymoons, as parents. It is to the sea that they were taken as children. It is to the sea that they return in old age, to the endless retirement villages.

Habit of a lifetime

And why not? The fact is that Sydneysiders have clung to the coastline rather naturally, shrugging off the priggish, cramped and tight-lipped spirit of the first British settlers and openly embracing the more sensual and hedonistic spirit of their Mediterranean environment. It would take a serious bloody-mindedness not to lap up the perfect skies, the sea breeze, the glorious mounds of prawns and oysters, the lathered bodies laid out on the sands and basted with oil like kebabs on a spit.

Under the Antipodean sun, more austere national traits succumb to the easy-going, tolerant, obsessively casual Sydney manner. It's no surprise to see a first-generation immigrant from Glasgow turn into a surfie overnight; the daughters of black-shrouded Muslim women lolling bikini-clad in the outdoor 'beer garden' of a pub; the sons of Puritanical Germans dilute the work ethic so they can spend a few days a week windsurfing.

In the same way, Sydney has been transformed from a sexually-closeted old maid to one of the world's most liberal-minded cities. Gay culture has exploded. In the 1960s, police agents of 'Bumper' Farell – a corrupt, devious chief of the Vice Squad – acted as decoys for homosexuals in the public toilets of Martin Place. Today, Sydney has taken over from San Francisco as the gay capital of the Western world, and the Gay Mardi Gras parade is the highest-attended event in the country, usually luring 600,000 to watch floats of fabulously-attired transvestites and lesbian nuns on Harley-Davidsons ('Dikes on Bikes'). Later in the year, the fabulously popular 'Sleaze Ball' attempts to overcome world records for partying – turning full circle from Sydney Cove's first convict debauch of 1788.

Orientation

Sydney may be vast in area, but most visitors will rarely stray out of a fairly compact zone. Major hotels cluster in the Circular Quay area, and that's the best place to understand the city's bizarre history and hopes for the future. It's also where harbour ferries all start and return, and one can easily spend a week just hopping around the waterway's many peculiar inlets and attractions. From the city's central zone (the Central Business District, or CBD), one can easily strike into the trendy eastern suburbs, then continue on the sea at legendary Bondi Beach. Manly remains one of Sydney's traditional seaside excursions; another is to stroll along the bush-lined harbour front (itself a national park) to Taronga Zoo.

Bondi Beach

Historical Highlights

Approximately 20,000BC The first Aboriginal people arrive in Sydney area; clans such as the Eora live by hunting and fishing, painting every sandstone outcrop with elaborate rock art.

1770 Captain James Cook lands at Botany Bay and raises the Union Jack, claiming the entire east coast of Australia for the British Crown. He passes by Sydney Harbour, but does not enter.

1788 The First Fleet arrives with 1030 people, including 548 male and 188 female convicts under command of Governor Arthur Phillip. Finding Botany Bay dry and unsuitable, the prison camp of New South Wales is set up in Sydney Cove; Eora Aboriginals greet them with stones and the cry Warra! Warra! (Go away).

1789 First convict hanged for gruesomely murdering fellow prisoner; his remains are placed in a cage on Pinchgut (today Fort Denison) as a warning to new arrivals. Occasional skirmishes with local Aborigines lead to Bennelong being captured to act as mediator.

1790 The colony nearly succumbs to starvation with the arrival of the ill-equipped Second Fleet; the settlers are too nervous to try any local plants or animals, which Aboriginals have been living from for millennia. An all-convict cast puts on a production of George Farquhar's comedy, *The Recruiting Officer*.

1793 The first free settlers arrive in the colony; ex-convict James Ruse begins first successful farm in Parramatta.

1797 The first Merino sheep are brought from South Africa.

1802 After four convicts are killed by Aborigines, a party is sent out to randomly 'punish the natives'. White settlement is pushed forward with 'a line of blood'.

1803 *Sydney Gazette,* first Australian newspaper, started.

1804 Irish convicts revolt in Castle Hill, attempting to seize ships in Sydney Harbour. The uprising is crushed, and nine leaders are hanged.

1808 Soldiers rebel against the heavy-handed Governor William Bligh, of *Bounty* fame, in the so-called 'Rum Rebellion' (rum being the main unit of currency in the colony).

1810–21 Visionary Governor Lachlan Macquarie begins to transform Sydney from convict camp to outpost of Empire. Ex-forger and architect Francis Greenway begins designing public buildings.

1815 Explorers Blaxland, Wentworth and Lawson find first path through the Blue Mountains, the barrier to western expansion, heralding Sydney's commercial expansion as a port.

1836 Visiting Sydney on the *Beagle*; naturalist Charles Darwin is fascinated by Australian fauna, and predicts grand things for British settlement (although Sydney he likens to a small London suburb). Free settlers begin to arrive in large numbers.

1840 Following pressure from free settlers, transportation of convicts to Sydney is abolished (some 150,000 passed through its gates, mostly being released after their terms). A colonial class system emerges: the Exclusives (English-born free setters – the gentry); Currency (Australian-born free settlers); Emancipists (ex-convicts); Ticket-of-Leave men (parolees).

1851 Gold is discovered near Bathurst in the Blue Mountains, starting Australia's first gold rush, with Sydney as its fountainhead. Fears of Russian invasion prompt the building of Fort Denison in Sydney Harbour.

1855 The first railway, between Sydney and Parramatta, commences operation.

1868 Attempted assassination of the Duke of Edinburgh while on a royal visit.

1880 The Garden Palace, built in the Botanic Gardens, hosts the southern hemisphere's first international exhibition. Sydney *Bulletin* magazine heralds literary boom in Australia: it pushes for an Australian Republic free of 'the cheap Chinaman, the cheap Nigger and the cheap European pauper'.

1891 Australian Impressionists of the Heidelberg School, Arthur Streeton and Tom Roberts, set up artists' colony in Mosman.

1900 Outbreak of bubonic plague causes large areas of Sydney's Rocks area to be razed.

1901 Antipodean states join federation as the 'Commonwealth of Australia'. Although Melbourne is the temporary capital, disgruntled Sydneysiders make sure that a new capital, Canberra, will be built halfway between their two cities. (Parliament is officially transferred to Canberra in 1927.)

1902 Women win the vote in New South Wales. Thanks to union movement, standard of living for Sydney workers becomes higher than British or American equivalents.

1914 Sydneysiders enlist en masse to fight in World War I; in the next four years, Australia suffers highest per capita casualties of any allied nation.

1919 Spanish influenza epidemic kills more in Sydney than four years of war casualties.

1921 D. H. Lawrence visits Sydney and is unimpressed: he finds it a cheap copy of London, 'as margarine is a substitute for butter'.

1928 At the Sydney Cricket Ground, local hero Don Bradman scores 452 not out against England, the highest-ever score in first-class cricket.

1932 Sydney Harbour Bridge opens at the height of the Great Depression; soon after, leftist Labor Premier Jack Lang is dismissed for threatening to default on war debt payments to Britain. Relations are not improved by England's bodyline bowling tactics in cricket test, aiming directly at batsmen.

1935 Luna Park, Sydney's grand harbourside entertainment centre, opens its gates.

1939 Sydneysiders enlist en masse to fight again in Europe.

1942 Japanese advance in the Pacific provokes recall of Australian forces from Europe; the fear of Japanese invasion causes a realignment with the US over Britain. Three midget submarines cause havoc in Sydney Harbour, torpedoing a ferry on which troops are sleeping. Nineteen men are killed.

1945 As a sign of return to peace, the first Sydney to Hobart yacht race is held.

1951 Australia signs the ANZUS defence treaty, aligning itself more closely with the US.

1954 Outpourings of support as Queen Elizabeth II visits Sydney show that sentimental attachment to the Mother Country is hardly dead.

1956 TV comes to Sydney, and with it US cultural influence.

1958 Work begins on Sydney Opera House.

1961 The last trams are removed from Sydney's streets; ownership of a car becomes every Sydneysider's sacred birthright.

1965 First Australian troops sent to Vietnam; skyscrapers begin to change Sydney's skyline.

1973 Sydney Opera House opens; Patrick White wins Nobel Prize for literature; Dame Joan Sutherland, La Stupenda, carries the banner of high art abroad as an upsurge in creativity hits Australian local scene. With the demise of the White Australia policy, Asian immigration begins to change the face of Sydney. 'Green bans' placed by building unions save Sydney's key historical districts from demolition.

1978 First Gay and Lesbian parade in Darlinghurst.

1980S Sydney takes over Melbourne's role as financial capital of Australia.

1988 Sydney is the focus of celebrations for Australian Bicentennial; Aboriginal activists lead protests against 200 years of white 'invasion'.

1993 Mass celebrations as Sydney beats Beijing in bid to hold the 2000 Olympics. Massive public building begins, plus real estate frenzy. Push for an Australian Republic gains pace.

1997 Last Royal Easter Show held in Randwick; key site is developed as Rupert Murdoch's Fox film studio.

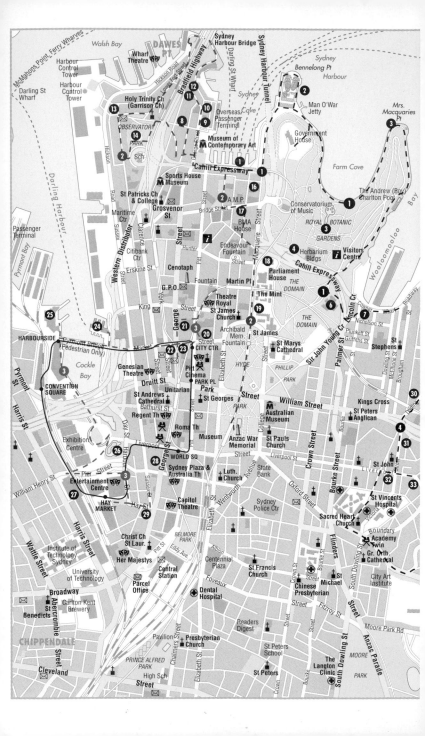

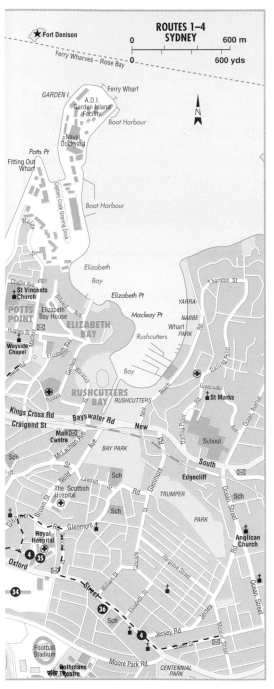

ROUTES 1–4
SYDNEY

0   600 m

0   600 yds

★ Fort Denison

Ferry Wharves – Rose Bay

GARDEN I.

A.D.I. Garden Island Facility

Ferry Wharf

Boat Harbour

Naval Dockyard

Potts Pt

Fitting Out Wharf

Boat Harbour

Captain Cook Graving Dock

N

W Ave St

Elizabeth Bay

Challis Ave

† St Vincents Church

POTTS POINT

Elizabeth Pt

Thornton St

Elizabeth Bay House

Billyard Ave

Macleay Pt

YARRA-NABBE

Hughes St

ELIZABETH BAY

Wharf PARK

Wayside Chapel

Macleay St

Elizabeth Bay

Gardens

Waratah

Rushcutters

Darling Point

Bay

Roslyn

RUSHCUTTERS BAY

RUSHCUTTERS

Beach

Greenoaks

Darling Point Rd

† St Marks

Kings Cross Rd

Bayswater Rd

New

Ocean Avenue

Ocean Ave

Craigend St

New

Mail Centre

Ave

McLachlan Ave

BAY PARK

Rd

School

Sch

Nelid St

Lawson

St

Sch

Glenmore Rd

South

Edgecliff

⊠

Brown St

Glenmore St

The Scottish Hospital

Sch

TRUMPER

Ocean Street

Sch

Glenmore Rd

Glenmore

†

Royal Hospital

4

35

PARK

† Anglican Church

Oxford

Street

William St

Cascade St

Hargrave Street

Elizabeth St

Jersey

Ocean Street

34

36

Sch

4

Jersey Rd

Queen St

Moncur Street

Football Stadium

Rothmans Theatre

Moore Park Rd

CENTENNIAL PARK

Sydney Opera House, Route 1

SS Bounty, Route 2

Chinese Gardens, Route 3

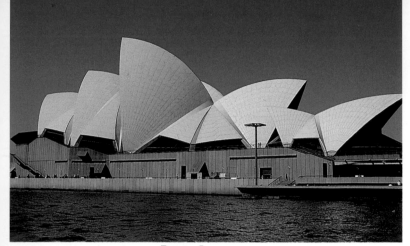

Sydney Opera House

Route 1

Harbour Promenade

Circular Quay – Sydney Opera House – Botanic Gardens – Mrs Macquarie's Point – Art gallery of NSW – Woolloomooloo (4.8km/3 miles) *See map, pages 14–15*

A stroll around the harbour shorefront is the obvious introduction for any new arrival to Sydney: the Opera House lures visitors like a postmodern beacon, and the walk around its environs provides a gentle pace for those wanting to get over their jet lag. Much of this tour involves a restful promenade through the Botanic Gardens, which includes a perfect lunch venue within (or you can simply pull up under a tree with a picnic). And so that the day is not purely hedonistic, the Art Gallery of NSW will provide an edifying preview of Sydney culture to come.

Circular Quay: a hive of activity

Start from **Circular Quay ❶**, the terminus for all harbour ferry trips. This was more or less where the first convict camp was set up in 1788; within a few years, it became the hub of Sydney's maritime life (and it was known, more correctly, as 'Semi-Circular Quay'). In the 1840s, some 150 sailing schooners would be berthed in the harbour, waiting to load and unload their goods at the wharves here; by the turn of the century, Sydney was the second port of the British Empire, and Circular Quay became devoted to local commuters (D. H. Lawrence in 1921 was amazed at the frenzy of water activity, with people 'slipping across the Harbour like fishes'). These days, 'the Quay' is a somewhat gaudy hubbub of activity, but the easiest place to find almost every service, from money exchange outlets to automatic banks and transport information.

Preceding pages:
Sydney Harbour Bridge

Apart from the hordes of commuters and tourists, the quay is a lively social scene, packed with buskers, peddlars and relaxing office workers from the skyscrapers towering nearby. Spend some time listening to an Aboriginal didgeridoo performance, or watching an elderly Italian craftsman build giant models of 18th-century ships. Embedded in the footpath are bronze memorials to writers from Henry Lawson to Barry Humphries, with quotes about Sydney. Note that on weekends, the number of visitors to the quay is usually greater than facilities can stand: mobs remain motionless around bizarre busking performances or queue at unappetizing take-away food bars, while the occasional pickpocket works the crowd.

Follow the waterline around Circular Quay (heading right as you face the water), along the functionally-designed **Promenade**, leading towards the Opera House. The little old brick kiosk (now the ★ **Sydney Cove Oyster Bar**) provides one of the best harbour views in Sydney – the ideal spot to watch the green and yellow ferries plough in and out of their berths, as well as faster Jetcats, water taxis and tour boats of every size taking passengers up and down the grand waterway. It's not hard to see why a relieved Captain Arthur Phillip, in 1788, described this as 'the finest harbour in the world, where a thousand ship of the line may ride with the most perfect security'.

Sydney Cove Oyster Bar

17

There's also the classic view of the ★★ **Sydney Harbour Bridge**, first symbol of Australian modernity. The largest single-span bridge in the world went up during the depths of the Great Depression as a symbol of hope in the future, much as the Brooklyn Bridge was in New York. As work went on, Sydneysiders dubbed it the Coathanger, the Toast Rack and the Iron Lung (the latter for the number of people given work on its construction, which kept Sydney breathing). Although the bridge was opened in 1932 – the ribbon was sensationally cut by a right wing paramilitary officer on horseback, stealing the honour from the controversial left-wing Premier Jack Lang – the last payment for the bridge's construction was only made in 1988. It has always been part of the city's mythology (legend has it that comedian Paul Hogan was 'discovered' working as a bridgeworker when he tried to talk a man attempting suicide from jumping). These days, despite dire predictions that rust is rotting it away from the inside, the bridge is still the major link between Sydney's northern and southern suburbs (an underground tunnel, opened in the early 1990s, provides some less picturesque assistance).

Sydney Harbour Bridge

At this point, the promenade splits into two levels as it enters the massive Opera House complex on **Bennelong**

Sydney Opera House

Point (named after the Aboriginal man captured here in 1789, and forced to be a mediator between the British colonists and local clans; for years he was a well-known figure on Sydney Cove, appearing in the cast-off jacket of a Royal Marine). Take the lower level of the promenade, which runs closest to the water's edge via outdoor restaurants and souvenir shops, all with magnificent harbour views. This is also where you'll find the ticket office for performances, and the starting point for guided tours of the interior. Different tours are offered every day, depending on performance schedules; they last for about an hour and cost $12 (but truth be told, the exterior is the great attraction here).

Begun in the 1960s, the ★★★ **Sydney Opera House** ❷ is without a doubt one of the world's most spectacular buildings (or as art critic Robert Hughes would have it, 'the biggest environmental site-specific sculpture south of the equator'). It was designed by the Dane Jorn Utzon after he won an international competition – although nobody at the time quite knew how it would be built. Without the aid of computers, it took nine years to even work out how to make its glorious white shells stay up. Costs escalated. Utzon became caught up in the petty-minded moneygrubbing of Australian politics, and resigned in disgust in 1966 (he has never returned to Sydney to see the finished edifice). A state lottery raised the necessary cash, and when the completed building was finally opened by the Queen in 1973, it had cost $102 million, or 14 times its initial budget.

But, although the acoustics in the concert halls are not all they could be and the seats are notoriously hard, nobody has ever complained about the price since. The Opera House became an immediate icon for Australia's newfound cultural independence. Today, Sydney without it is unthinkable. Far more than a house of opera, it includes several stages, presenting concerts, dance, drama and gallery exhibitions in a year-round schedule.

Spend an hour or so poking around the Opera House's famous white-tiled sails, then watch the real sails on the harbour from one of the tables at the **Front Forecourt** where, on weekends, musical and theatrical performances are held. There are good views of Sydney's priviledged North Shore suburbs from here, as well as of **Fort Denison**, the tiny yellow sandstone fortress-island in the middle of the harbour. Originally known as Pinchgut (as the narrowest point of the inlet), this was once where the whitening bones of executed convicts were left in cages, as a warning to new arrivals. (The first man to be hung on its shores reputedly gazed around him from the gibbet and said calmly: 'Well it certainly is a nice harbour you 'ave 'ere'.) In the 1860s, with the gold rush underway in the Blue Mountains, local fears of a Russian invasion led to the fortress being built, with a half dozen cannons aimed, rather forlornly, at the Sydney Heads. Every day, the One O'Clock Cannon is still fired.

From the Opera House, follow the waterside walkway around to **Farm Cove**, one of the prettiest inlets in the harbour. Site of the first vegetable garden in Sydney (begun without much success in 1789), it is now given over to the sumptuous ★★ **Royal Botanic Gardens** (daily 7am–sunset). The imposing iron gateway beyond the Opera House jetty is the main entrance to this vast, voluptuous collection of Antipodean flora and fauna, which includes some truly majestic Moreton Bay figs and a merry band of sulphur-crested cockatoos which get drunk on natural alcohol in fruit and swoop low over picnickers.

Botanic Gardens statuary

Discreetly crowning the headland as you enter the gardens are the fairy tale turrets of **Government House** (Friday to Sunday 10am–3pm). Built between 1837 and 1845 as the official residence of the New South Wales Governor, this is Sydney's most sophisticated example of Gothic Revival architecture. Further along the hillside crest behind Government House, are the Governor's original stables and servants' quarters. They were even then considered excessively designed; today they house Sydney's **Conservatorium of Music.**

Government House

Return down to the water's edge, at the beginning of the gardens, then follow the splendid walkway along the sculpted curve of the inlet. Apart from their natural beauty, the gardens are Australia's oldest scientific institution. Within these 30 hectares (75 acres), 7,500 species are on display, with the National Herbarium of NSW conducting valuable research on native plants. As you wander, take

Morton Bay fig tree in the Botanic Gardens

the occasional detour back into the gardens to gape at the massive fig trees and manicured lawns. At the middle point of the curve, follow a path back amongst the sculpted lakes and exotic fronds to the **Botanic Gardens Restaurant** ❸, an excellent eatery with a curved open-air veranda that's virtually hidden in greenery. You can't do better than this for your first lunch in Sydney.

Further back from the restaurant lies the **Sydney Tropical Centre** ❹ (daily 10am–4pm). Native plants are housed in a giant glasshouse pyramid; maintained at a steamy temperature, rainforest plants from Northern Queensland and Kakadu thrive. If you have time, other paths lead to a Rose Garden, Herb Garden, Australia's First Farm Exhibition, Palm House, Fernery, Succulent Garden and Visitor Centre. Lastly, an event that has quickly become a Sydney tradition is the outdoor Shakespeare-in-the-Gardens productions. Held on summer evenings, it is designed so that the trees themselves become part of the theatrical stage, festooned with coloured fairly lights to create a magical atmosphere. The feeling is enhanced by rogue possums looking for picnic food amongst the audience, while the gardens' resident bats make guerrilla strikes from overhead.

Lady Macquarie's Chair

20

Continue around the harbour to **Mrs Macquarie's Point** ❺ (also known as 'Lady Macquarie's Chair'). The site was named after the wife of Sydney's most ambitious early governor, who liked to sit here and gaze out at the harbour; her stone seat, cut into the cliff, still has the best view in Sydney. A colonial-era inscription marks the site, which has always been a favoured picnic spot.

From here, take the lower path along the next bay, Woolloomooloo. This route provides views of **Garden Island Naval Dockyard** – a naval barracks since 1888, it was expanded in the 1940s to help in the war effort against the Japanese. At the time the first European graffiti in Australia was discovered here – the initials of a trio of Marines carved in 1788 (Aboriginal activists say white settlers have been busily defacing the country ever since). If there's an American warship in port, you'll probably also see an anti-nuclear demonstration going on around here.

Next to the docks are the historic Woolloomooloo **finger wharves**, which once served passenger boats and are now being restored as apartments. On a hot day, you can even take a dip en route at the **Andrew (Boy) Charlton Swimming Pool**; this salt water baths was named after the local boy who won an Olympic gold medal in 1924, at the tender age of 16.

Continue over the noisy Cahill Expressway to the ★★ **Art Gallery of New South Wales** ❻ (daily 10am–5pm). This imposing edifice is crowned with the celes-

Andrew Charlton Swimming Pool

Young gallery goers

tial names of Da Vinci, Michaelangelo, Boticelli and the like, although not one of these artists is actually represented in the collection. What the gallery does have is the finest grouping of Australian art in the country – colonial through to contemporary – as well as an extensive collection of Aboriginal art, housed in the new Yiribana Gallery. Curators are proudest of their Tom Roberts classic *The Golden Fleece* (1894), showing shearers in the bush; their set of Drysdales; and their Pukumani burial poles from the Tiwi Islands, north of Darwin. Also well worth seeing are Brett Whitely's modern visions of Sydney Harbour.

21

David Moore sculpture

Stretching out in front of the Art Gallery is **The Domain**, another welcome expanse of open greenery in the city area. From the 1890s it was used as a sort of 'Speaker's Corner'. Although occasional soapbox orators continue to harangue scattered onlookers on a Sunday afternoon, the Domain is only really crowded during the regular summer concerts, where Chardonnay vintages and opera tenors are the main points of debate.

Cut back across the expressway and head down the stone stairs, into the suburb of **Woolloomooloo**. The area has been rapidly developing into prime residential real estate. A favourite meal for many Sydney generations has been at the **Woolloomooloo Bay Pub ❼** (the one ablaze with Australian flags), which specializes in huge plates of fresh seafood in a relaxed 'beer garden' setting.

Harry's Café de Wheels

An even more beloved institution is the colourful 'pie wagon' – **Harry's Café de Wheels** – which is permanently parked a little further down on the wharf side of this traffic-crazed street. Harry's has been serving the traditional Aussie meat pie in all its glorious variations (try the pie'n'pea floaters) to working folk since 1945 – as the fascinating photo gallery in and around the wagon will attest.

Historic Sydney

The Rocks – Phillip Street – Macquarie Street (4.8km/3 miles) *See map, pages 14–15*

International Passenger Terminal

Rocks revival
Jeff Koons's 'Flower Dog' outside
the Museum of Contemporary Art

For this walk, start again at Circular Quay: as the landing point for the first sea-weary collection of convicts and British Marines in 1788, this was where the city of Sydney had its implausible beginnings. From the quay, it is possible to explore the key elements of Sydney – and thus Australia's – early history, which Mark Twain described as being such a rip-roaring and colourful affair that it might have been made up entirely.

Leaving the quay's tourist frenzy behind, head around the harbour towards the looming **International Passenger Terminal**. As late as the 1960s, almost all Australians left for foreign shores from its giant bulk. The last P&O liner for Portsmouth departed in the early 1970s, but today, the occasional cruise ship has begun to reappear. Just back from the waterline, pass through the squat yellow **Museum of Contemporary Art**. This blunt 1950s version of deco style architecture was once home to the Maritime Services Board, which ran Sydney's waterways; its outdoor café is, for the art crowd, the ultimate lunch address on a sunny day. (At $11 entry fee, the MCA is quite pricey for its modestly-sized collection, but you can pass directly through the museum's foyer without paying, cutting to George Street.)

Behind these two monumental structures begins Sydney's best preserved historic district: ★★★ **The Rocks**, named after the sandstone bluffs from which the first con-

victs cut golden bricks for Sydney's gutters and public buildings. This was also the first prison-ghetto of the young colony, where prisoners were piled up in fleabag doss-houses run by Marines sodden with rum.

Today, the Rocks' pubs and terraces are glossily painted and polished, full of up-market stores selling Aboriginal art and tourist souvenirs. But even quite recently, the Rocks was still considered one of Sydney's most squalid and dan-gerous corners, a Dickensian warren where the rum was laced with tobacco juice and the larrikin (hooligan) 'razor gangs' preyed on the unwary (a bubonic plague outbreak in 1900 being a particular low-light of its history). Most urban planners could think of nothing better for the Rocks than to wipe the blot from the face of the city. Shame-fully enough, as late as the 1970s, developers were given permits to level the whole historic area – only to be saved when the left-wing builder's unions, led by activist Jack Mundey, refused to start work. This was the beginning of the 'green bans' that saved whatever was atmospheric about Sydney's cityscape.

The best place to start a walking tour of this rich 19th cen-tury maze is **George Street**. Although currently occupied by clothes designers, opal jewellers and sheepskin sou-venir shops, the buildings themselves have fascinating his-tories. At number 127, the glitzy 'Australian Craftworks' is housed in the former **Police Station**, which dates from 1882: the solid, iron-doored prison cells are still perfectly intact, but they now showcase the delicate silver and pot-tery work of local artisans. The history goes even fur-ther, since the police station was built on the site of Sydney's first general hospital.

George Street and the former Police Station

Walk through the **Captain Tench Arcade** – named af-ter an unusually humane Marine officer, whose corre-spondence is a major source of data for the convict era – to **Nurses Walk**, for a typical example of the Rocks laneways. Brass plaques provide fascinating details of each pedestrian-only stretch. Head forward to the **Suez Canal** – the name is a play on its real purpose as a 'Sewer's Canal' in less salubrious days. It is now home to a cluster of court-yard cafés, as it narrows up to Harrington Street. Just around to the right is the **Gumnut Tea Garden** – the pre-sent occupant of **Reynolds Cottage**, one of the earliest houses in the Rocks, built and occupied by the blacksmith and his large family – with a preternaturally serene dining garden.

Argyle Street is the most famous of the Rock's streets, thanks to the striking **Argyle Cut** – the slice of roadway, at the top of the street, which was hand-chipped out of a solid sandstone hillside by convicts in the 1840s. The pick

The Orient Hotel

Cadman's cottage

marks of the chain gangs are still easily identifiable. This is also where to find the classic ★ **Argyle Centre** ❽ – a shopping centre housed in enormous restored wool stores, which were built from 1826 around an atmospheric cobblestone courtyard. For nearly a century, it housed wool exports and valuable imports (such as rum); any trader who failed to pay his custom duties had his goods auctioned off in the courtyard. The Argyle Centre now houses some of Sydney's most stylish restaurants and designer boutiques, but the wool store's original wooden beam interiors are virtually unchanged, providing a dramatic, almost Gothic setting.

Head back to the corner of George and Argyle streets, where the **Orient Hotel** continues to be a rowdy pub (in true Rocks tradition). Crowds on Friday and Saturday nights spill out onto the footpaths, and the Orient is probably the busiest pub in Sydney on New Year's Eve, when drunken hordes take over the Rocks and bellow out favourite songs.

Down the stairs at the Harbour Forecourt is ★ **Cadman's Cottage** ❾ (Monday 10am–3pm, Tuesday to Friday 9am–4.30pm, Saturday and Sunday 11am–4pm), the oldest building in Sydney – now the office of the National Parks and Wildlife Service. Built in 1816 as a naval barracks, the four-room cottage was soon taken over by the freed convict John Cadman and his family. Cadman worked as a coxswain, or helmsman, of government craft. When he lived here, the high-tide waterline of Sydney Harbour washed just two metres below his front door (landfill has since pushed it back 50 metres). Today, this is the place to come for information on the Sydney Harbour National Park, which includes Fort Denison, a great deal of the harbour foreshore, and Goat, Clark and Shark islands. Tours leave for Fort Denison at noon every day.

Beside the cottage (the entrance is back up the stairs) sits the old ★★ **Sailors' Home** ❿ (daily 9am–5pm), built as a doss-house for seamen – a morally decent alternative to the seedy Rocks brothels they were tempted by. It has recently been renovated, and is now home to the Rocks Visitors Centre, with an efficient information desk and lavish exhibitions about the area. On the top level is a cubicle recreating the original sleeping conditions for a sailor guest (allowing no room for visiting prostitutes, presumably).

From here, cut back up to **Rocks Square** – part of a tranquil walkway, which is backed by a pretty row of early terraced houses. These now house off-beat stores, specializing in items such as antique prints and maps of Sydney, all connected by overhead paths and interspersed with courtyard cafés. On tiny Atherden Street are a number of tiny, quaint private residences and the **Westpac**

Museum, with its monetary memorabilia, including the recreation of a bank in the 1890s.

Around the corner is the ★ **Merchants House Museum** ⓫ (Wednesday to Sunday 10am–4pm), a Greek Revival sandstone and cedar house which has been restored to its 1850s splendour. It is most popular for its Australian Childhood Collection, which includes items such as an old Rocking Kangaroo and an early toy Harbour Bridge. Children simply follow a blue line on the floor through displays. The exhibition also includes artwork from classic Australian literary children's books, such as May Gibbs's *Snugglepot and Cuddlepie*, Norman Lindsay's *Magic Pudding* and the comic-book character Ginger Meggs. On weekends, the stretch of George Street near here becomes a hive of activity thanks to **The Rocks Market**.

Walk down Customs Officer Stairs to the open waterfront, where ★ **Campbell's Storehouses** ⓬ have been turned into a string of outdoor seafood restaurants to lure foot-weary tourists. Eleven of the 12 original storehouses remain from the private wharf of merchant Robert Campbell, built in 1839 for his imports from India. The antique pulleys used to raise the cargo now seem like deliberate design features on these trendy restaurant facades. Just in front of the storehouses, the *SS Bounty* is generally moored. Built for the Mel Gibson/Anthony Hopkins film version of *Mutiny on the Bounty*, it now sets out every day for cruises of the harbour.

Campbell's Storehouses

25

SS Bounty

Follow the front past the Park Hyatt Hotel, where the stunningly located, palm-fringed little **Dawes Point Park** is, not surprisingly, popular with wedding photographers.

Head under the bridge to **Lower Fort Street**. This takes you through a quieter residential neighbourhood, known as Miller's Point, with terraced houses dating back to well before the turn of the century. This whole area was once the domain of waterside workers, or 'wharfies', whose union was one of the most powerful in Australia. Their families joined together in a tight-knit, supportive community whose members rarely left the neighbourhood.

In the 1950s, the introduction of containers in shipping largely broke the union's power, and led to the area's decline. Still, many descendants of the wharf workers continue to live here.

The **Hero of Waterloo** pub remains a favourite of locals, despite the new flood of tourists who come to see its convict-chipped walls, the stones for which were taken from the Argyle Cut. Back when Sydney was a Conradian port, sea captains would have drunken sailors drugged and pushed through a trap door in the floor. They would only wake up to find themselves pressed as crew members on an already departing ship. In the even more atmospheric corner of Miller's Point, the **Lord Nelson Hotel** ⓭ has

The Lord Nelson

Susannah Place

the honour of being the oldest pub in Sydney. Its first ale was poured in 1834; today, an inviting parlour, with a log fire for winter, makes it an excellent place to stop for a Sydney beer.

Stroll down Kent Street and climb the stone stairway known as **Agar Steps** (after Thomas Agar, an early resident). **Observatory Hill** was originally the site of a fortress, Fort Phillip, where officers planned to defend in case of a convict uprising; today it is a favoured picnic spot, with fine harbour views. The ★ **Sydney Observatory** ⓮ (Monday to Friday 2–5pm, Saturday and Sunday 10am–5pm) is a wonderful-looking manor house, with twin copper observation domes that look to be straight out of H.G. Wells. After Fort Phillip was demolished in the 1840s, the site was used for a 'time-ball tower': for decades, Sydneysiders knew that the big black ball would drop at precisely 1pm (the same time as the cannon was fired on Fort Denison). The tower was quickly expanded into a well-equipped observatory, including equatorial and transit telescopes. Today, the observatory still opens at nights for star-gazing.

Observatory Hill

Sydney Observatory

Stroll around to the rotunda in the front of the park, then take the Bridge Stairs tunnel down to Gloucester Street, which runs past the classic Australian Pub to ★★ **Susannah Place** ⓯ (January, daily 10am–5pm, February to December, Saturday and Sunday only 10am–5pm). This valuable collection of terraces dates back to 1844; apart from escaping the bubonic plague demolition that ravaged the Rocks in 1900, the buildings have a history of continued domestic occupancy. Inside, a small museum shows changing living conditions by highlighting the renovations made to the building over time. There is also a turn-of-the-century grocery store, which sells uniquely Aussie foodstuffs that have been used for generations, from Billy Tea to lollies.

Mission Stairs takes you all the way back down to Nurses Walk in the heart of the Rocks. This is a good opportunity to have lunch or afternoon tea – there are plenty of small cafés and eateries along George Street, as well as in Circular Quay – before starting the second half of the Historic Sydney walk.

For this leg, head up **Phillip Street** at the opposite end of the quay. This has always been the 'official' part of the city, home to lawyers, politicians, judges and juries.

The ★ **Justice & Police Museum** ⑯ (January, Sunday to Thursday 10am–5pm, February to December, Sunday only 10am–5pm), although only with limited opening, is a colourful introduction to Sydney's criminal underworld. It is housed in the original Water Police and Court buildings, built in the 1850s and boasting fine sandstone architecture and iron lace detail. The museum includes all grisly memorabilia from the notorious waterfront gangs, including murder weapons and knuckledusters. There are accounts of Sydney's most heinous crimes, and a haunting selection of mugshots. Naturally, other rooms are devoted to the harsh Victorian judicial system under which they were tried. On occasion, visitors to the museum can even go through a mock-trial themselves; you'll be sentenced by a zealous colonial judge, and even spend a night in prison.

Justice & Police Museum

At the corner of Bridge and Phillip streets is the new ★★ **Museum of Sydney** ⑰ (daily 10am–5pm), whose postmodern design went up on the site of the first Government House. During excavation, labourers turned up a wealth of domestic and military artefacts from the earliest colonial period. These objects, and the foundations of Government House itself, can now be seen under the museum's glass floor; others are incorporated into the imaginative multi-media installations, which include holographic ghost stories on Level One.

On display in the foyer is the actual foundation plate laid by Governor Phillip in 1788 to commemorate the landing of the First Fleet. It was lost until a telegraph lines worker uncovered it in 1899. The museum's outside courtyard shows the outline of Government House, and is enhanced by a striking sculpture, which looks like a forest of totem poles. The *Edge of the Trees* is intended to symbolize the meeting of Aboriginal and European peoples. The Sydney Museum places considerable focus on the lives of the Eora people, the city's original inhabitants, in an attempt to make up for generations of indifference to Aboriginal history.

Museum of Sydney: 'Edge of the Trees'

As it was in colonial times, **Macquarie Street** is the heart of official Sydney. Once just a gloomy row of public buildings, they are now accepted as important examples of early architecture, and have been renovated to appear at their best.

The **State Library** ⑱ (Monday to Friday 9am–9pm, Saturday and Sunday 11am–5pm), is an excellent resource for anyone interested in Australian history. It can be counted on to have some fascinating exhibitions, and the book shop is excellent. In the foyer of the Mitchell Wing – in the grand old sandstone building facing the Botanic Gardens – is a beautiful inlaid floor, depicting an early Dutch map of Australia taken from the 1640 voyage of Abel Tasman.

Parliament House and the **Sydney Mint** are like Georgian twins, with their attractive colonnaded verandahs; they stand on either side of the even more imposing **Sydney Hospital**. This was originally the site of the convict-built Rum Hospital, so named because its overseers were granted the valuable right to resell imported rum. It's a Sydney tradition to rub the nose of *Il Porcellino*, the brass boar that sits out in front, for good luck. The Mint once turned gold into bullion and currency. It now houses a museum on the subject and visitors can mint their own souvenir, a replica of an 1855 coin.

Along this stretch, ★★ **Hyde Park Barracks** ⑲ (daily 10am–5pm), stands out as one of Sydney's most popular attractions. Designed in 1819 by architect Francis Greenway, who started life in Australia as a convict having been banished by the English for forgery, the building was used to house convicts when they first arrived in the colony. Some 150,000 unfortunates are said to have passed through its doors. Today, exhibits relating to 'the System' include a recreation of the cramped canvass-hammock sleeping quarters, where some 600 convicts would spend the night at the same time. Paying guests can now make reservations for the night in these hammocks – one of Australia's more unusual hotel experiences – while a computer database allows visitors to look up their convict ancestry. The museum also has a very good outdoor café within the authentic gravel-floored compound.

At the end of Macquarie Street lies **Hyde Park**. Here you can relax by the **Archibald Fountain** or continue through a canopy of green to the impressive art deco **Anzac Memorial**, which is reflected perfectly in the foreground pool. It was built to commemorate the slaughter of Anzacs (Australian and New Zealand Army Corps) in Gallipoli in 1915 – a military disaster which Australians, rather perversely, saw as the birth of the nation ('baptism in blood' being the preferred metaphor). Inside is an exhibition that relates the history of Aussies at war.

New Parliament House

Rum Hospital plaque

Hyde Park's Archibald Fountain

Route 3

Sydney's CBD

Monorail tour

Martin Place – Centrepoint Tower – Strand Arcade – Queen Victoria Building – Darling Harbour – Chinatown (3.2km/2 miles) *See map, pages 14–15*

Sydney's Central Business District – the 'CBD' as everyone refers to it in shorthand – is an oddly anonymous hodge-podge of glass skyscrapers and architectural styles from the last two centuries, all squeezed onto a street plan that was drawn up in Georgian times. Slithering its way around the main shopping areas of the CBD is the controversial **Monorail** – which, despite endless protests that it turns Sydney into a Disneyland and promises by politicians that it will be torn down, shows no sign of slowing. Although it runs through only a handful of stops, the monorail has become very useful as a way to explore the inner city, and is also the easiest way to get to **Darling Harbour**, the largest of the city's modern developments.

Start off on foot at the pedestrian mall of **Martin Place** – the office-workers' Rialto, where every lunchtime rather hokey live entertainment is staged in the concrete amphitheatre. From here, descend into the modern shopping arcades of the **MLC Centre**, devoted to super-expensive international designer names, and emerge on the other side in King Sreet next to the **Theatre Royal**, home of the big Broadway-style musicals. Now you can join the throngs on the **Pitt Street Mall**. Although not much to look at, this shopping walkway is probably ground zero for Sydney's CBD – which makes it an apt location for the ★ **Centrepoint Tower ⑳**. This controversial, needle-like structure is regarded as a phallic eyesore by many

Centrepoint Tower

*George Street facade and the
Queen Victoria Building*

Sydneysiders, but it does have incredible views from the summit. There's also the inevitable revolving restaurant and a less expensive café and bar. Tickets for the elevator ride to the Observation Deck are sold three escalator flights up from street level.

Pitt Street and **George Street** are this part of the city's main arteries, with a number of shopping arcades connecting them. For a pleasant contrast to all the modern architecture, stroll through the historic ★ **Strand Arcade** ㉑. Built in 1893, it instantly became the height of Victorian chic in the Southern Hemisphere; today, shoppers still peer genteely into expensive shop windows, whose coloured glass patterns match the floor tiles within. The Strand Hatters is the place to pick up your Aussie Akubra, with or without crocodile-teeth band.

Emerge onto bustling George Street and walk one block south to the grandiose ★★ **Queen Victoria Building** ㉒. This Romanesque-inspired structure covers an entire block and is Sydney's most impressive commercial building. It was built during the depression of the early 1890s as Sydney's main produce market; for years it remained derelict, until being lovingly restored in the 1980s. Today, it houses the city's leading collection of chic stores. The stained glass windows, Byzantine arches and plaster ornamentation have made the QVB, according to Pierre Cardin, 'the most beautiful shopping centre in the world'.

Returning back up Market Street (towards Centrepoint Tower), make a quick stop at the **State Theatre** ㉓. Sydney's best-loved theatre was built in 1929 as a cinema, and was considered then to be the finest in the world (well, at least by Sydneysiders). Today, after years of neglect, the venue has been restored to its full splendour – from its Gothic foyer and grand staircase, to the vast auditorium with its 20,000-piece chandelier. Before each performance, the Wurlitzer organ still rises from below the stage. While used for many events, the State is considered by many to be the special home of the Sydney Film Festival.

At the corner of Pitt Street is the entrance to the upstairs Monorail station called 'City Centre'. Purchase a Monorail Day Pass for $7 so you can get off and re-board all day.

Darling Harbour

The first stop is 'Darling Park', on the eastern side of the vast entertainment complex ★ **Darling Harbour**. Originally called Cockle Bay, because the European settlers would collect molluscs here, the area was later officially named after Ralph Darling, the seventh Governor of New South Wales. Throughout the 1800s, Darling Harbour was the 'back-door' to Sydney, where trading ships docked. For much of the 20th century, the whole area was little more than an industrial wasteland. Then, for the 1988 Bicentennial, a grand reclamation project was conceived.

Darling Harbour is now a brash, shiny and unashamedly touristy collection of shops and restaurants, with an Exhibition Centre, Conference Centre and a bunch of luxury hotels thrown in for good measure. While the family carnival atmosphere is not to everyone's taste, Darling Harbour does have a number of specialised attractions that makes it well worth a visit.

The first monorail stop, Darling Park, is the access point to ★ **Sydney Aquarium** ❷ (daily 9.30am–9pm). This

Outside the Aquarium

is the largest in Australia, with exhibits from around the country and two spectacular underwater walkways – glass tunnels around which fish swim. The sharks, of course, steal the show as they cruise in slow motion directly over visitors' heads, revealing their several layers of razor-sharp teeth. The Aquarium is also worth a visit for the Great Barrier Reef exhibition and the 'Touch Pool', a rare opportunity to carefully handle marine invertebrates such as starfish, sea urchins, tubeworms, even a giant hermit crab.

To reach the opposite bank of Darling Harbour, either catch the monorail (to 'Harbourside') or walk across **Pyrmont Bridge**. This is the world's oldest electrical swingspan bridge, which still opens regularly for all vessels over 14m (46ft) tall. While most of the bridge is made of the Australian hardwood ironbark, the central swingspan is made of steel. When it opened in 1902, it used electricity long before it had been developed to light Sydney's streets. It now has great views, especially of the famous Dragon Boat Races held here every April.

The vast shopping expanse on the other side of the bay is known as **Harbourside**. Apart from a wall-to-wall selection of restaurants and shops, this is the site of the unique ★★ **National Maritime Museum** ❷ (daily 9.30am–5pm). This place covers everything that is even vaguely related to the sea, recounting a time when Sydney's life as a port was its main *raison d'etre*. Imaginative exhibits start with accounts of the early exploration of Australia, then move through the early development of the shipping industry and the waterside workers union movement. There is fascinating memorabilia from the golden era of cruise ships – which, until the 1960s, were really the only means for Aussies to reach the outside world – and displays covering early 'beach culture', complete with Edwardian swimming cossies (costumes). Other prize items include the actual *Australia II* racing yacht, whose controversial winged keel wrested the America's Cup from the US for the first time in the early 1980s; a figurehead of Lord Nelson; and an entire lighthouse. Intact vessels include a fragile Vietnamese refugee boat which survived a hellish voyage to Australia in the 1970s; the *Spirit of Australia*, the fastest boat in the world, which set the world

With Nelson at the National Maritime Museum

water speed record in 1978 at 511kmph (317 mph) using an aircraft engine; and a Royal Australian Navy destroyer, *HMS Vampire*, moored outside at the dock. In front of the museum is the *SS South Steyne*, the most famous of the old Manly ferries from the 1930s. It was also 'The Biggest Ferry in the British Empire', continuing in service right up until 1974 and was quite an impressive sight, ploughing through the harbour with pistons pounding.

Behind the gaudy, glass-covered entrance arch of the **Harbourside Marketplace** – with its New Age sculptural tribute to man and beast living in harmony under the sea – lurks a baffling conglomeration of souvenir, gift and clothing shops (around 200 of them at last the count). The Darling Harbour complex goes on to offer an assortment of family-orientated activities. The **Panasonic Imax Theatre** insists it has *the* biggest movie screen on earth. It's hard not to notice the garish **Sega World** – identified by a giant lime green pyramid – which is an indoor family theme park (topics: Past, Present and Future). The **Ettamogah Pub** is a bloated caricature of a country pub from an Australian cartoon series, while the **Rainforest Café** comes complete with waterfall, forest fernery and a menu based on 'natural' ingredients. Last but not least is the long-awaited **Sydney Harbour Casino**, where Sydneysiders can now flock to squander their life savings.

Fortunately, Darling Harbour offers a respite from the commercial hubbub in the ★ **Chinese Gardens** ㉖ (daily 9.30am–5pm). Also called the Garden of Friendship, this is a compact example of traditional southern Chinese landscaping. Donated by the city of Quandong, Sydney's sister city in China, it borders on the edge of Chinatown. With its delicate pavilions, ponds, weeping willows and cascades, the enclosure is now valued as one of the most tranquil corners of Sydney.

Chinese Gardens

Sega World theme park

Another edifying attraction close to Darling Harbour is the ★ **Powerhouse Museum** ❷ (daily 10am–4.30pm). The building was the former power station that supplied the electricity to Darling Harbour's swingspan bridge, as well as Sydney's trolley system in 1902. The museum is now devoted to the applied arts and sciences in Australia. Its early collection was originally housed in the magnificent Garden Palace in the Botanic Gardens – the setting for the 1879 International Exhibition on Industry and Invention, which was destroyed by fire in 1882. After major renovations, the Powerhouse Museum opened in 1988 with avant-garde interactive displays. Continually growing in size, the Powerhouse today works on an almost overwhelming scale, with vast spaces covering just about anything relating to human achievement: including science, space technology, transport, manufacturing industry, information technology, decorative arts and fashion.

From here, stroll into ★★ **Chinatown** ❷. Dixon Street is the main pedestrian thoroughfare, where dragons parade at Chinese New Year. Here, and on parallel Sussex Street, are dozens of sumptuous food halls with excellent and inexpensive take-away food, as well as huge restaurants serving authentic cuisine from every corner of Asia. Try the Golden Century or East Ocean on Sussex Street for the best Chinese. A great Sydney tradition is heading down to Chinatown on weekends for Yum Cha (whereby you select small plates of food from passing trolleys, held at mid-morning; many of the best restaurants have long waits). Thanks to the quality of the ingredients, the Asian food here is usually superior to what can be had in Asia. At each end of Dixon Street stands a decorative gateway, guarded by mythical Chinese lions.

33

Yum Cha in Chinatown

At the southern end of Dixon Street is the site of another Sydney tradition: **Paddy's Market** ❷. Every Sydney university student can remember the Saturday mornings spent trudging through its cacophonous rows of greengrocers in search of the city's cheapest veggies. Paddy's has been around since 1869, with only one short break of five years when the building needed to be saved from collapse. It was thought to have been named after the first working class merchants here, who were predominantly Irish. Today, Paddy's is just a small section of the much larger compound called Market City. The big draw card here is its dirt-cheap stalls: bargain-basement clothing can be found, but the place is only happening on the weekends.

When you're ready to leave, there's a convenient monorail station – **'Hay Street'** – just around the corner. Since the monorail runs in a circle, you can stay on board for a while to get a bird's eye view of the streets you've just covered on foot.

Lion tamers

*Darlinghurst's Gay Mardi Gras
in full swing*

Route 4

Hip Sydney

Kings Cross – Darlinghurst – Oxford Street – Paddington – Queen Street (4km/2½ miles) *See map, pages 14–15*

(Note that Saturdays are particularly auspicious for this walk: that's when Paddington market is held, and the gallery scene is at its most active).

In many ways, it is the assortment of 'inner-city suburbs' (as they are paradoxically called) that show Sydney at its most genuine. In the late 19th century, row after row of terraced houses were thrown up as cheap worker's accommodation – usually with small gardens, tight porches and elaborate iron lace decorations. Several families at a time squeezed into these places in the early 20th century, and as soon as they could, most moved to the more spacious suburbs in search of the Aussie dream. But from the 1970s, gentrification began apace, turning many dismal old addresses into the height of fashionable living.

*Kings Cross:
a haunt near the station*

Although these days it is something of a mixed bag, the obvious start to a tour of Sydney's cool environs is its erstwhile bohemian centre, **Kings Cross**. Just hop on the underground to Kings Cross Station and take the Darlinghurst Road exit. When you emerge near the corner of **Darlinghurst Road and William Street** ㉚, be prepared for a wave of shabby but rather harmless sleaze.

In Victorian times, this part of Kings Cross was elegant and tree-lined; in the 1920s and 1930s, it was Sydney's artistic hotbed; but the Vietnam war and drug boom turned it into the city's red-light strip. A jaunt up the main drag

('Darlo Street') late on a Friday and Saturday night leads you past a parade of smack-addled prostitutes, drunken yobbos, wide-eyed backpackers and pimply adolescents from the Western Suburbs ('westies'). Unless you have a fascination with cheap strip joints and fast food parlours, such an excursion is without doubt Sydney's least attractive night jaunt. Meanwhile, on the nearby footpaths of traffic-clogged William Street, regal transvestites cluster outside luxury car dealerships.

Yet curiously, to either side of these main streets lie some of Sydney's most charming and fashionable neighbourhoods. Cross the William Street overpass into **Victoria Street** (the road on the left side of the old fire station). This is the suburb of **Darlinghurst**, chic centre for Sydney's blossoming fashion set. The first two blocks of the street seem like wall-to-wall coffee bars, where you'll feel seriously out of place if you're not wearing dark shades and a scowl or pout. **Bar Coluzzi ③** is perhaps the most famous of these hangouts, where a selection of locals – from body-pierced kids to ageing Italian grandfathers – plop themselves down on mushroom-like stools and stay for hours. Across the street is the back entrance to a wonderful little café **Le Petit Creme** whose very French owners prepare Sydney's best breakfasts in lightning speed. Also here on Darlinghurst Road is **Govindas**, where guests enjoy an all-you-can-eat vegetarian meal then recline on pillows before a feature film presentation.

Pavement life in Victoria Street

As you stroll down **Darlinghurst Road**, check out the trendy eateries that you might want to return to after dark (here the restaurants and cafés *are* the scene). **Burgerman** is famous for his gourmet burger variations, while a range of new noodle bars are doing a brisk trade as the latest thing in gourmet snack food. **Morgan's** is a more up-market boutique hotel catering to the well-preened young business crowd; its multi-tiered front bar seems to serve as a showcase for the fashion industry. The grand dame of the strip runs the quirky old Hungarian café, **Una's** – for nearly a generation, Sydney's bohemia has been staying alive on her legendary Veal Paprika.

Continuing onwards, **Fez Café ㉜** is a confirmed cool Middle Eastern scene, offering its customers street-side cushioned seats on which to display themselves. In its more discreet location ★ **bill's ㉝**, (yes, ostentatiously a lower case 'b') is another civilised Darlo institution. It specialises in modern Australian breakfast and lunch dishes (at half the price of comparable places) and has a large communal table strewn with the latest magazines – an informal hodgepodge, and a great place to meet people. If you can't squeeze in at bill's, pass the time at **Blue Spinach** – a designer and recycled clothing shop diagonally opposite. Returning to Victoria Street, **Fishface Café** is much more

The Fez Café

Hip Oxford Street

A literary venue

than your average fish'n'chips with its exotic Asian variations, while the **Green Park Hotel** is one of the oldest pubs in the area, where you can while away an afternoon over a few games of pool, accompanied by a well-chosen jukebox number.

Continue along the ominous stone fence, called simply 'The Wall'; it's a known meeting place (and pickup venue) for locals, and the perimeter of the old **Darlinghurst Gaol**. The path finally emerges onto ★★ **Oxford Street**, perhaps the key promenade of hip Sydney: this is the Antipodean version of New York's East Village, where you'll find the coolest attitudes and most fashionable haircuts, all carried along in swathes of black leather. Oxford Street's coolness dates back to the late 1960s, when it emerged as the main artery of Sydney's gay culture (a thriving society that has now outstripped San Fransisco's in size and energy). Every March, the Gay Mardi Gras lures more than 600,000 Sydneysiders from all corners of society to watch the climactic, flamboyant parade down Oxford Street (a million more Aussies catch it on TV). In this tolerant city, the mayor and MPs make sure they're in on the act alongside the Dikes on Bikes and floats showing, say, a gay, black Captain Cook.

Oxford Street and its side alleys are home to the latest designer stores and cheapest restaurants in Sydney. As you stroll east, the street enters the suburb of Paddington and slowly transmutes into a more self-consciously trendy thoroughfare. In quick succession come the landmark gay pub the **Albury** (seen in the flick *Priscilla, Queen of the Desert*), a cluster of art cinemas, **Mambo** (a store devoted to a famous Australian design label), followed by the discerning booksellers of **Berkelouw** and **Ariel**, sites of readings, book launches and literary events of all kinds. From here, walk on the left side of Oxford Street to take in curious boutiques like **Sweet Art** (a couture cake shop where icing sculpture has been taken to its highest form) and **Coo-ee Aboriginal Art Gallery** full of Koori-made gifts, fabrics, books and posters.

Victoria Barracks ㉞ (parade and tour Thursday 10am), takes up nearly 30 acres (12 hectares) of inner-city real estate and is, surprisingly, the largest collection of Georgian architecture in Australia. It was built from 1841 to 1848 using locally quarried sandstone, and the excellent design has kept it in continuous use since then. Even today, it is still thought to be one of the best examples of its kind in the world. The museum, in a former jail block, presents Australia's military history. The residential neighbourhood across Oxford Street was built to house the stonemasons, carpenters and quarrymen who supervised the chain-gangs working on the barracks back in the 1840s.

A number of simple sandstone cottages are still nestled here, now occupied by the rather well-to-do.

This is the beginning of **Paddington** proper. The terraced houses here are the most impressive in Sydney, the iron-lace more intricate, the back streets the most leafy and seductive. Of course, it was not always so. Before the barracks were established, this was a barren wilderness of sandhills and dry scrub. Soon Paddington sprang up as a working-class district. Without building regulations, the first terraced houses of the 1880s were very narrow and connected in long, cramped rows – definitely budget accommodation. Usually they would be shared by several families, one family to a room. By the 1920s, terraces were regarded as little more than sorry slums: Sydney's remoter suburbs offered larger homes with sizeable plots of land for gardens, regarded by most as the epitome of the Aussie dream.

By the 1960s, 'Paddo' became a textbook study in urban gentrification. Artists, writers and students moved in to the rundown neighbourhood and began renovating. A few cafés and bars sprang up. Soon, others became more aware of the benefits of inner-city living, while Sydney began to realize that terraces were its most distinctive architectural style. Prices jumped, and most of the artists, writers and students were forced out (the art dealers and advertising execs, however, stayed).

Today, prestigious art galleries and interior design studios are hidden down every laneway in Paddington, so keep your eyes peeled. A good start is **Walker Lane**, home of ★ **Hogarth Galleries/Aboriginal Arts Centre** ❸❺ (Tuesday to Saturday 11am–5pm), which has a highly regarded collection of traditional and urban Aboriginal Art. At the bottom of **Liverpool Street**, turn right into **Glenmore Road**, where there are some particularly grand terraces (numbers 97 and 99, for example). Sydney's best art galleries are located amongst this maze of tranquil back streets, and another full day could be spent visiting these alone. They are generally open from Tuesday to Saturday from 11am to 6pm, although the general public tends to do the rounds on Saturdays. A few of the best are: **Sherman Galleries** (1 Hargrave Street), which shows contemporary painting and drawing, and has a sculpture garden; **Roslyn Oxley9 Gallery** (Soudan Lane, off 27 Hampden Street), Sydney's major showcase for contemporary artists; **Josef Lebovic Gallery** (34 Paddington Street), specialising in vintage photography, including important Australian photographers such as Max Dupain; **Holdsworth Galleries** (86 Holdsworth Street), representing well-established Australian artists.

Back on Oxford Street, **Juniper Hall** looms as one of Sydney's most splendid buildings. Built in 1826 as the

Leafy Paddington

37

Gallery exhibit

Juniper Hall

Paddington Market

Relaxing after shopping

home of a successful gin merchant, this National Trust-listed property is the oldest standing example of a Georgian villa in Australia. For years the National Trust used it as its own offices, but it is now owned (perhaps symbolically, for Sydney) by real estate agents, who only deign to open their doors to the public twice a year.

From this point, Oxford Street devotes itself to serious shopping, with fashion boutiques becoming thicker on the ground, and more expensive, as you head east. Scattered between the clothes stores are plenty of eccentric speciality stores, offering a good cross-section of Sydney's commercial creativity.

At the centre of the strip, in a leafy churchyard, is the location of one of Sydney's most popular weekend attractions: ★★ **Paddington Market** ㊱ (Saturday only). Once a week, the area in and beyond the church is turned over to 'the Bazaar'. When the sun is out, half of Sydney seems to turn up in search of bargain clothes from young designers, unique jewellery and handicrafts of every description. The carnival atmosphere spills out from the churchyard: buskers, fortune-tellers and comedians set up shop on the fringes of the market, while, across the street, visitors parade their recent purchases at every outdoor café. You can while away a whole day here just in the act of people-watching. For an injection of culture, check out the **ACP (Australian Centre for Photography)**, which shows cutting edge work, or the more intimate **Stills Gallery**, also for contemporary photography.

At the end of Oxford Street, on the far right corner, is the entrance to **Centennial Park**, the largest and most natural expanse of Australian flora in the city, with some lovely lakes and picnic spots. Bicycling and horse-riding are popular, as is roller-blading. The boots are available for rental nearby, so watch out for rank beginners careering down the paths.

Where Paddington ends, Woollahra takes over – unlike its nouveau riche neighbour, this is a suburb that has always been exclusive. Head down **Queen Street**, now known as Sydney's Antique Row, where one can acquire the finer things in life for princely sums. **Charles Hewitt**, at 30 Queen Street, specialises in antiquarian prints, framing and fine cabinet making, while further down the street, **Tony Ward's Printique** specialises in Australian colonial maps (have a look at his exquisite decorative botanicals).

If this flamboyant display of Old Wealth is all too difficult to swallow, stop in for a drink at **Bistro Moncur** at the bottom of Queen Street – its trendified interiors are oddly comforting, reminding you that hip Sydney is not too far away.

Route 5

The Bondi experience

Classic beach Sydney

Bondi – Tamarama – Bronte (3.2km/2 miles) *See map, page 40*

Sydney's east is lined with one glorious, surf-pounded ocean beach after another – but the most famous is certainly ★★★ **Bondi** (pronounced Bond-*eye*).

A taxi from the city will cost you around $15, around half that from Paddington (ask to get off on the corner of Campbell Parade and Lamrock Avenue; needless to say, pack your swimming gear). You can also get to the beach by public transport: take the Eastern Suburbs railway to Bondi Junction, then hop on the 380 bus, which follows the old tram route through sleepy back streets lined with the first apartment buildings in Sydney, erected in the 1920s in a humble Art Deco style. Bondi Beach is also a suburb, the place where the Australian dream blossomed within sight of the Pacific. These days, however, the final destination feels anything but suburban as you round the headland at the end of Bondi Road and plummet down Campbell Parade towards a horizon filled with blue.

For a century, this great arc of sand has played a crucial part in Sydney's self-image. It was at Bondi in the late 1880s that the first Aussie 'cranks' braved the ocean – breaking an ancient law that forbade swimming between sundown and sunset as indecent. Many were arrested, tipped off by local residents. The breakthrough came in 1903, when a Waverly clergyman and a respectable bank clerk – following the highly-publicised lead of Manly (*see page 57*) – defied the ban. Despite a newspaper reporter's opinion that the pair had made a 'disgusting spectacle of themselves', crowds of Sydneysiders soon followed suit.

Watch the currents

In 1906, the world's first lifesaving club was set up on Bondi's shores. Twenty years later, crowds of up to 100,000 people were reported visiting Bondi on summer's days; a tramline was built to shuttle the hordes at breakneck speed from the city (creating the enduring Sydney phrase, 'as fast as a Bondi tram'). Duke Kahanamoku of Honolulu introduced Aussies to surfing here – and the first to take it up was a woman, although males soon made it their own macho preserve. With its wide golden sands, ragged sandstone headlands and reliably fine rollers, Bondi Beach had become the most potent of Sydney's icons.

The place is at its best, not surprisingly, in summer. Activity kicks off at dawn, with the joggers on the promenade, bodybuilders by the shore and surfies catching a few waves before work. Sun-worshippers arrive by 9am, closely

Sun worshippers

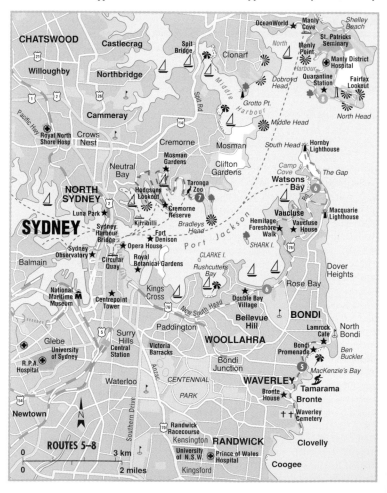

ROUTES 5–8

followed by busloads of Japanese tourists. The Bondi Pavilion opens up, selling ice-creams and souvenirs, picnickers arrive with their fish'n'chips, and the activity continues until well after dark, when the lovers take over.

But even in winter, Bondi is well worth a visit for its clear air, brilliant light and the famous walk from the south end of the beach, along the sandstone headlands to Tamarama and Bronte. The views are glorious and you'll be rewarded with a string of excellent cafés at the end.

Start your walk from the good old **Lamrock Café**, located halfway up the rise of the main beachfront thoroughfare, Campbell Parade. This Bondi institution has sweeping views of the beach, fine people-watching potential, and serves the best 'flat white' (strong coffee with milk) in town. If the Lamrock is full, the **Bondi Tratt**(oria), only a few steps up the hill is also a great vantage point.

The Lamrock Café

Campbell Parade is a motley string of 1930s-era storefronts. In the mid-1990s, talk of a 'Bondi Renaissance' began as the suburb unexpectedly leapt to new heights of fashionability: real estate prices went through the roof, and strings of chic 'New Australian' restaurants opened on the Parade's northern end, adding pockets of sophistication to the time-tested bedrock of take-out food shops. Another recent improvement has been reclaiming a great swathe of kerbside parking space in favour of outdoor café tables, adding a touch of the Riviera to the promenade. But despite it all, Campbell Parade hangs on to its raffish, sand-gritted personality – and most Sydneysiders, really, would have it no other way.

Aficionados on Campbell Parade

But before heading to the Parade, check out the beach itself: cross the street and descend the hill to the **Bondi Promenade**. Of late, the atmosphere in Bondi has become more like Venice in Los Angeles or Miami's South Beach, with exhibitionism the order of the day. Rollerbladers are out in full force, skateboarders have their own runs, and body-builders cluster at outdoor bars. Of course, the water wins the day here, and swimming is more pleasurable in Bondi than ever. In the late 1980s, Sydneysiders were scandalised by reports of high sewerage levels at the beach; rumours flew of swimmers encountering used condoms, hypodermics and 'brown torpedoes' in the surf. A local outcry led to a massive cleanup, and Bondi now has amongst the cleanest, glassiest waters in Sydney. It is well set up for day visits: for $2, you can leave your valuables in a locker at the shop on the beach (beneath the viewing tower). As at all Sydney beaches, you should swim 'between the flags' – the red-and-yellow banners that indicate the calmest waters, surveyed by life-savers. As a general rule, the northern end of Bondi is more family-oriented, while the southern end tends to be younger.

On the Bondi Promenade

Bondi Pavilion mural

At the centre of the promenade, the **Bondi Pavilion** has had numerous facelifts, yet still manages to show its age. You can call in for the free public changing rooms and cold showers, but take a minute to look around. The rambling old edifice is carved up into confusing nooks and crannies, which are randomly hired out for any community purpose. The souvenir shop has a fun collection of black-and-white postcards of earlier days on Bondi Beach; there's a café with piles of gourmet lunch sandwiches and tables connecting up to the central courtyard. Take a look at the faded murals of lifesavers – a tribute to the Bondi spirit. The open space is used for the occasional ethnic music festival.

Connected to the Pavilion is **Bondi Surf Bathers**, the lifesaving club founded in 1906. The club had its greatest moment in 1938, when a giant wave struck on a summer's day and washed 200 people out to sea. Five were lost, but the others were saved by a massive effort. There is a **statue of a lifesaver** outside the Pavilion commemorating this and other grand efforts.

Lifesaver statue

42

After a swim, continue along the beachside promenade to the northern end of the beach, where there is a toddler's wading pool and a short walk out on the rocks. Legend has it that the giant boulder here was washed up one night during a fierce storm. Although this might be pushing things a bit far, you should be careful of freak waves, which have 'taken' fisherman by surprise and washed them out to sea. Leave the beach by ascending the stairs and pathway beside the R.S.L. Club, up to the street.

This end of Campbell Parade is where the newer, trendy eateries such as **Biboteca** and **Aqua Bar** have sprung up, and where the coolest Bondi locals gather. Follow the parade back towards the Lamrock, passing by a splendid row of the Art Deco apartment buildings Bondi is famous for, before arriving at the looming, white monstrosity of the **Swiss Grand Hotel**, which was constructed only after local protest actually prevented a higher building.

The Bondi Pub

More authentic is the **Bondi Pub**, across the street. There is more genuine Bondi history in its repainted stucco balconies, beer-sodden carpets, pool tables and clattering poker machines than any other site. Long before the days of modern Australian cuisine and random breath testing, wasted lovers would emerge from its raucous doorways at closing time to collapse on the sand, and the night air would echo with the cries of amorous trysts.

At the centre of the main drag are Sydney's most famous **fish'n'chips shops**. Far from your basic battered-shark-and-greasy-potato-scallops, they now dish up a vast array of fresh local catches and will even grill fish rather than deep-fry. Retire for a picnic on the lawn across the street for the traditional Bondi feast.

Once replete on Barramundi and Chardonnay, it's time to consider the famous coastal walk to Bronte. Walk south along the beachfront promenade towards the looming headland. The stairs take you up to the roadway for a stretch, then left alongside the **Bondi Public Baths** – home of the Bondi Icebergs, the local winter swimming club (whose members admittedly face less of a challenge than, say, those in Coney Island in New York, where waters are barely above freezing). Just after the clubhouse, follow the stairs and concrete pathway down to the rocky coast. The golden sandstone cliff face here is beautifully eroded into colourful layers and intricate patterns (in stark contrast to a rusting abstract sculpture that is mounted here, of a winged bicycle heading out to sea). The rocky cove has also become a favourite spot, it seems, for individuals to quietly practice yoga, chant or silently philosophise. Meanwhile, joggers hurtle along the pathway at breakneck speed, so keep an eye out for sweat-streaming juggernauts.

The Bondi Public Baths

Sweeping views of Bondi Beach can be had from the walk out to the point. Keep an eye out for a (rather faint) **Aboriginal carving** of a large fish or shark; for 20,000 or so years, the whole Bondi area was an Aboriginal 'workshop' for manufacturing chips, splinters and points. You'll notice the bars of exercise equipment here – the first installment of a 'fitness circuit' set up at intervals along the route. Rising to the top of the grassy headland, you can see one beach after another gnawed into the seashore heading south. The most prominent point is **Clovelly**, whose 19th-century **Waverly Cemetery** takes up most of the real estate. Australia's great bush balladist Henry Lawson is buried there, while an Irish Memorial commemorates a doomed 1798 rebellion of Irish convicts at Castle Hill.

43

As you round the curve into the next inlet, **Mackenzies Bay**, there's a steep view down into the swirling turquoise

Mackenzies Bay

The café at Tamarama

waters, where surfers bob about on their boards like corks in a giant churn. The path then sinks down past a headland, to **Tamarama**, a very pretty little beach that has long been favoured by the young and beautiful, who lay themselves out like sausages on a barbecue, rarely bothering to fling themselves into the rough surf. Take the route via the Surf Lifesaving Club and down the steps to this pristine expanse of white sand. There's a stretch of grassy parkland behind the beach, as well as a very pleasant outdoor café. Cross through the park and take the steps back up to the roadway, so you can continue following the coast southwards (Tamarama Marine Drive changes its name to Bronte Marine Drive as you round the headland into the next bay).

Bronte Beach and its rock pool

From here, the path descends again to **Bronte Beach**, the ostensible goal of the walk. Bronte is much larger than Tamarama and has calmer waves, making it a more family-orientated spot; there's also a naturally-enclosed rockpool at its southern end, ideal for little kids. There's a walkway out to an ocean-side swimming pool and rocky point, although the path ends there.

Sweeping back from the beach, Bronte Park is one of the lushest and shadiest stretches of green on Sydney's foreshore. This was once the private estate of **Bronte House**, a 19th-century mansion located on the hill above. Head directly away from the sea, where a secluded path leads back through the park; the flanks of the hillsides narrow towards a small stream and culminate in a charming waterfall, which was originally landscaped as part of the estate's gardens. The route brings you to the back of Bronte House, now under private lease; its eclectic exterior (the dream of first owner Mortimer Lewis, who was an architect) can only be seen by peering over the fence.

A Bronte café

Follow the curving road back down to the beach – where you'll find the row of trendy little cafés that have recently put Bronte back on the map. Many Sydney families swear by the **Bronte Chippa**, for fish'n'chips. This is followed by wall-to-wall eateries, jam-packed with outdoor tables, including a Brazilian spot and **Tarifa** – 'a mostly healthy café', where being seen is at least as important as the food. For the most relaxing experience, however, take your picnic across to the park, where there are plenty of quaint old-style wooden picnic shelters and barbecues for a dose of classic Aussie beach culture.

If this hike hasn't tuckered you out, you can continue further south, following Bronte Road, to **Clovelly** and **Coogee** beaches. The latter has recently been given a major facelift, although the mall-style atmosphere has ensured that it will never quite compete with the organic mix of shabbiness and chic that make visiting Bondi and Bronte such a peculiar pleasure.

Route 6

Wndow display in exclusive Double Bay

Ritzy Sydney

Double Bay – Hermitage Foreshore Reserve – Vaucluse House – Watsons Bay – The Gap (6.4km/4 miles) *See map, page 40*

Any quaint, anachronistic pretensions Australia has of being a classless society crumble when confronted with the areas covered on this walk. Ever since early colonial days, the harbour regions of the eastern suburbs have been the bastion of the 'Exclusives' (in fact, the social division may date back to Day One of white settlement, when the convicts and rank-and-file Marines were packed off to huddle in the west of Tank Stream in Sydney Cove, while the officers retired to relative comfort in the east). Today, while the North Shore has no shortage of millionaires, Sydney's most dazzling stretch of uninterrupted opulence remains here on the opposite bank, extending from Elizabeth Bay around the harbour to Watson's Bay.

Clustered here are most glamorous Old Money addresses, the international jet-setting crowds with their designer labels, the private clubs, private schools and most importantly – the grandiose mansions with private harbour frontages. While it's not easy to infiltrate this exclusive society on a permanent basis, Sydney at least allows democratic voyeurism: there are many excellent harbour walks, beaches, shops and restaurants where one can join the Beautiful People indulging their whims.

Bay chic

To start this walk, take a taxi for breakfast in **Double Bay** (ask for the Sir Stamford Hotel). On the drive along winding New South Head Road, you can almost hear the sound of real estate values climbing. Keep an eye out for the first

Sir Stamford Hotel

of the picturesque harbour inlets that indent this coastline like toothmarks: Rushcutter's Bay, whose waterfront park and Yacht Club announce the exotic East. Still, it's not until you're over the rise and into **Double Bay** that you've really *arrived* in swanky Sydney. Double Bay is synonymous with Old Money and all its (occasionally comical) pretensions in Australia – although, since World War II, a large contingent of Central European immigrants have made the grade, adding to the blood lines and keeping the many designer shoe shops and hair salons in business. While Double Bay's celebrity status took a serious beating in the 1980s, a number of recent developments – such as the new Ritz Carlton Hotel – have put the gloss back on its reputation for display.

To get into the swing of things, settle in for an expensive breakfast at the outdoor café of the **Sir Stamford Hotel**, which has turned into the nerve centre of Double Bay. The crowd here looks like the cast of a big budget movie on their five minute break. The younger denizens sport preternatural suntans, dark glasses and cellular phones glued to their ears, modelling themselves on trendsetters from *Beverly Hills 90210*; but it is the Double Bay matrons who are truly legendary in Sydney for their snootiness and vulgarity, their flamboyantly expensive yet oddly tasteless clothes, their face-lifts and bleached hair ('mutton dressed up as lamb' is one cruel Australian expression that can be bandied freely here). Still, although the Double Bay burghers would like to pretend they are on Fifth Avenue, there is a tangible sense of uncertainty in the air, as if everyone needs to huddle together for security from the rest of Sydney. (If you can't get a table at the Sir Stanford, try the nearby Dee Bees or the Blue Oyster for that instant, rather dubious 'you're-in-the-club' feel.)

After breakfast or a cappuccino, take a stroll within the area. The compact **'Double Bay Village'** is triangular in shape, bordered by New South Head Road, Bay Street and Cross Street. Head first to **Transvaal Avenue**, a *cul de sac* of tiny turn-of-the-century cottages that have been converted into couture outlets for big name designers. **Cross Street** is home to the Ritz Carlton hotel, and the serious shoe contingent of Raymond Castles, Hermans and Varese Shoes; there's also the **Georges Centre**, an elegant hive of speciality stores. Dotted within the rows of expensive boutiques are tiny courtyards and laneways containing excellent European delicatessens and gourmet landmarks such as Bon Bon Chocolates and Bay Street Patisserie. Coffee is excellent at any of the European-style cafés, but the big draw card to Double Bay remains fashion, both Australian and international. The list of names on **Bay Street** alone includes Harry Who, TSE, MaxMara, Gary Castles, Maria Finlay, Carla Zampatti, John Serafino

Transvaal Avenue

and Saba. Jewellery and housewares are represented by the likes of Hardy Brothers, Christofle, Limoges Porcelain and Sheridan Australia.

To get away from it all, hail a taxi and request Bayview Hill Road in posh Rose Bay. Only five minutes away, this small lane runs alongside the Gothic **Kincoppal-Rose Bay private girls' school**, one of the most exclusive in Australia. But through a little marked pathway at the bottom of the lane begins the **Hermitage Foreshore Scenic Walk**, which runs along a narrow strip of harbour-fronted wilderness extending all the way to Vaucluse.

The hour-long stroll through this natural reserve provides magnificent harbour views; behind you looms the occasional majestic mansion, such as Strickland House. Shade is provided by characteristic Port Jackson Figs, and there's plenty of idyllic rest stops: grassy areas for picnics, sandstone outcrops as viewing points, even intimate swimming beaches to freshen up.

The trail ends up with the old-fashioned seaside charm of ★ **Nielson Park** in Vaucluse. This is a popular swimming and picnic spot with a tangibly Mediterranean family ambiance. Elderly Sicilian men play leisurely chess games in the forecourt in front of a quaint beachfront kiosk, which now houses a very good Italian seafood restaurant. A shark enclosure protects a large, calm swimming beach – Shark Bay. The view looks across to an undeveloped stretch of the North Shore, while water traffic gently plies up and down the harbour. Behind the beach is an historic parkland, once the estate of Greycliff House, which is hidden on the headland.

Stroll through the avenue of huge old trees and out of the park onto Coolong Road. This runs through **Vaucluse,** one of Sydney's most prestigious suburbs, and into the back entrance of ★ **Vaucluse House** (Tuesday to Sunday 10am–4.30pm). This magnificent estate was owned by the statesman, poet and explorer William Charles Wentworth from 1829–53. He was the son of a thief and highway robber who made good: apart from being a member of the first expedition to cross the Blue Mountains, Wentworth had an influential vision of Australia not as a penal dumping ground but 'a new Britannia in another world'. He pushed for a representative government, the formation of Sydney University, the colony's first newspaper, *The Australian*, and fundamental civil rights such as trial by jury.

A visit to Vaucluse house provides a fascinating insight into the domestic life of the 'bunyip aristocracy' – the first Australian-born upper class. Start in the well-equipped kitchen and cellars, with their original plaster ceilings and hooks for hanging cured meats. The drawing room occupies the oldest part of the house and still shows the orig-

47

Italian restaurant in Nielson Park

Vaucluse House

inal floral wallpaper; it was here that the New South Wales Constitution Bill was drafted in the 1830s, giving the colony a degree of independence. The upper floors are the most atmospheric, with the family sitting room and bedrooms which accommodated all ten of the Wentworth's children. Finally, the gardens are amongst the most charming in Sydney; strolling beneath the exotic fronds, you can imagine the genteel afternoons the Wentworths once spent on the front veranda as a cool respite from the Australian summer. Things were not always sedate. When Governor Darling, one of Wentworth's enemies left Australia in 1831, this was the site of a 4,000-guest party, ending with fireworks that spelled 'down with the tyrant'.

This is a good time to have a rest and a bite to eat. Hidden within the inviting palm-filled grounds of Vaucluse House is the elegant **Tea House** – a popular luncheon spot for generations of Sydney folk, with its tinted glass panes and gentle breezes evoking a bygone era. The menu today however is strictly modern Australian. You can also have more modest tea and scones.

The bridge at Parsely Bay

From here, call for a taxi and request Watson's Bay. For those who are feeling more energetic, it's about a 40-minute walk, with a great swimming spot on the way. Follow Wentworth Road around to Fitzwilliam Road, then onwards to picturesque **Parsely Bay**, with its tall banks connected by a pedestrian suspension bridge. This is a great place for a dip. On the other side of the bridge, the exclusive crescent curves around to Hopetoun Avenue. Turn left down the Palmerston Street pathway – past an early colonial street marker – and you've arrived.

The busy **Watson's Bay Pub** has, without much doubt, the finest outdoor 'beer garden' in Sydney. The view runs across moored yachts all the way back to the city skyline; this is also possibly Sydney's best sunset-watching location, retaining the last golden light longer than any other spot on the harbour.

Doyle's

Next door to the pub is **Doyle's**, a fish restaurant that has become a Sydney institution (it was the first to elevate local fish preparation above the oil-soaked, beer-battered level). Today, Doyle's boasts prices to match its fame. Long lines of customers gather every night (no reservations are taken), while local yachties still bring their putt-putts up to the beach, and stagger in for a plate of Barramundi and bottle of Chardonnay. Still, the sad truth is that Doyle's quality no longer lives up to the hype: you can now get better seafood, more cheaply, in lots of other places, although without the hubbub and panorama. (Sydney insiders pick up their fish'n'chips at the take-away store on the pier and retire to the park next door: the view is just as good and, frankly, so is the food.)

From the pub, it's a stiff hike up Pacific Road towards **South Head** at the mouth of Port Jackson, but worth it for more incredible views. This swathe of natural bushland falls within the HMAS Watson Military Reserve; take the path to the **Naval Memorial Chapel**, which has a spectacular view (through a glass window) of North Head and the Pacific Ocean.

From there, turn southward along the sheer cliffs of ★ **The Gap**, a favoured suicide spot for desperate Syndeysiders. A spectacular fall ends in fierce ocean-beaten rocks below. The path includes the **Dunbar's Anchor**, taken from a migrant passenger ship whose wreck here was Australia's worst peace-time maritime disaster. During a storm in 1857, the Dunbar's captain incorrectly decided that the Gap was the entrance to Sydney Harbour (which is, of course, 500 yards further to the right). He drove the boat directly onto the cliffs. There was just one survivor, a small crew boy who was tossed onto a ledge in the cliff face, and 121 passengers perished. **Jacob's Ladder** is the name of the narrow cleft where the lucky escapee was winched to safety.

Follow the trail from Gap Park into **Signal Hill Reserve**. Before the signal station was built in 1848, a flag would be raised from this location to warn the colony whenever a ship was entering the harbour. The trail follows high coastal scrub, usually whipped by fierce ocean winds. The southerly view from here includes the majestic series of headlands jutting out into the Pacific, stretching past some of Sydney's most famous ocean beaches, such as Bondi. Last stop is the pretty, twin-domed **Macquarie Lighthouse**, a replica of the country's first lighthouse, which was built on this site in 1818. The entrance is from the street side, where a bust of Queen Victoria graces the door.

Jacob's Ladder

Queen Victoria

Dunbar's Anchor

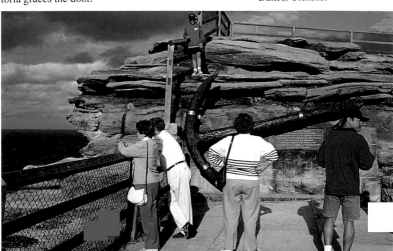

Affluent Neutral Bay

Route 7

Harbour hopping by ferry and foot

Neutral Bay – Cremorne Point – Mosman – Taronga Zoo (3.2km/2 miles) *See map, page 40*

Although the vast majority of Sydneysiders now live far from its shores, in red-roofed suburbia, the harbour triumphantly remains the visual and spiritual focus of the city – its spine, lungs and heart, as it were, all rolled into one. After all, without its harbour, Sydney would not exist. Thanks to the harbour's grand expanse, the city was able quickly to outgrow its convict origins and become a thriving trading outpost in Britain's maritime empire. Indeed, for most of the 20th century, Sydney's main role was as a port; it was only in the 1950s that shipping began to disappear.

Since the 1988 Bicentennial, there has been a massive revival of interest in the waterfront – as a backdrop for Sydney's leisure industry rather than trade – and a veritable boom in harbour traffic. Pleasure cruisers have appeared in many peculiar forms, including hire-by-distance 'water taxis'; a replica of the *Bounty*; a New Orleans-style paddle steamer; and even a Chinese junk. But despite all the new competition, the green and yellow harbour ferries, which stolidly plough in and out of Circular Quay, remain arguably the world's most pleasant form of commuter transport. These cheap, often antique boats can take you to almost every corner of the harbour (although the itineraries can seem to first-time visitors as difficult to figure out as the London Underground).

For the classic day excursion, the following walking route – which is connected by popular, easy-to-find fer-

One of the cherished harbour ferries

ries – follows the harbour through the most beautiful areas of the North Shore, and includes the most dramatic views of the city itself.

To start off, take the Neutral Bay ferry from Circular Quay (it leaves every 10 minutes or so, and fares are only $1.60). This ferry route stops first at **Kirribilli** wharf, situated directly across from the Opera House. The name is an Aboriginal word meaning 'place for fishing', and every morning dozens of locals still gather here with their hand lines. Perched in regal splendour on Kirribilli's lush, landscaped headland, you can see **Admiralty House**, built in 1843 as home for the British Admiral in charge of the Pacific Squadron. Today, it is the Sydney residence of the Governor General; the Queen's anachronistic representative in Australia has one of the finest homes in the country, much to republicans' chagrin. Somewhat less grand is the adjacent **Kirribilli House**, under whose Gothic gables the Prime Minister resides when he is in Sydney.

Neutral Bay

51

The ferry then turns into **Neutral Bay**. In the early days of the colony, merchant ships from foreign shores were obliged to anchor here, just in case a war had started on the other side of the globe and they turned out to be spies for Britain's enemies (after all, it could take nine months for news to arrive from Europe of a conflict). Today, Neutral Bay is one of the most affluent addresses in Sydney. There are three wharves in the bay, but stay on the ferry until the last of them – **Kurraba Wharf**.

Take the steps up past the three apartment houses called, oddly, **Once Upon A Time**. Architect W.A. Crowle built this eccentric architectural arrangement in 1936; it has become a landmark for Sydneysiders ever since, partly because of the buildings' mysterious chateau-like exterior, but mainly for the sign by the entrance gate, read by generations of commuters: 'Live peaceably with all, so shalt thou lead a happy life thyself'.

Hodgson's Lookout

When you reach the top of the stairs, turn right and follow Kurraba Road a short distance to the point. **Hodgson's Lookout** is a small, three-tiered park with the first of some incredible views back across the harbour to the city. Continue on to Shell Cove Road, then follow it to the right. The homes of **Shell Cove** mostly have expansive perimeter walls and vast driveways, indicating serious money; they also run right down to the water, so you can't see the fronts of these formidable estates until you're on the other side of the cove.

Continue into Honda Road and then right again towards the bay. (Note that this entire harbourside route follows as close as possible to the water – so if the streets sometimes seem confusing, you can't exactly get lost.) Here you'll find a tiny garden outlook, and the inviting entrance

to ★ **Cremorne Reserve** – which includes the prettiest stretch of walkway along the entire harbour. This is natural bushland scenery, smack in the heart of a city of 4 million people.

Meandering close to the lapping harbour waters, the Cremorne path is flanked by pink gum trees alive with native birds; on occasion, there are glimpses of spectacular harbour mansions to be spied through the foliage (one starts to gaze longingly up at the private balconies at this point, imagining the views of lucky residents). The panorama soon encompasses the entire majestic cityscape – one of the scenes recognisable from hundreds of tourist promotions. This is also an idyllic picnic spot. To the left of the park, poised above the waterline, is **McCallum Swimming Pool**: little known even to most Sydney folk, you can swim and sunbathe here with the best view in the city.

Cremorne Point

For those who wish to limit the amount of walking, there's a ferry wharf here that will take you ahead to Mosman Wharf, thereby cutting out 40 minutes on foot. Still, try and resist the temptation: the energetic will be rewarded. Climb the stairs opposite the wharf to the very tip of **Cremorne Point**, where the reserve continues rich with the aroma of native flowers. The pretty lighthouse here is used by ships coming into Sydney Harbour; seen from far outside the Heads, it lines up with another lighthouse to indicate the safest route for navigation.

The path continues around **Mosman Bay**. An exclusive hideaway packed with expensive yachts, it actually started life as a whaling station in the 1830s, run by a scurrilous old trader named Archibald Mosman. Today, the pathway passes through a swathe of beautifully landscaped ★ **Mosman Gardens**, the result of tireless volunteer work by local residents Lex and Ruby Graham. Begun in 1959, they are now dense with native plants and lush tree ferns, which cascade down the steep bank like the Hanging Gardens of Babylon. The indefatigable gardeners are commemorated by a plaque, and their handiwork recognised in 1984 with a special award by the National Trust.

Mosman bay and a trail through the gardens

The path becomes more rustic as it crosses the undeveloped inlet, fording a stream and rounding a cliff face before finally arriving at the **Mosman Rowing Club**. If they don't have a private function, you can stay for a bite or a drink on their open-air deck. It's a classic 'yachtie' scene, where the sound of yachts motoring carries across the water from the marina and mingles with the clink of beer glasses. The deck is a good place from which to watch the lumbering Mosman ferry manoeuvre with apparent ease into this tiny inlet, past all those fragile, expensive yachts.

Following the curve of the waterline, on the eastern side of the bay, is a valuable remnant of colonial architecture. Now a scout's hall, the squat sandstone **Barn** was built by Archibald Mosman himself in 1831 as a storehouse for his whaling enterprise. As the writer Jan Morris mused: it 'powerfully suggests to me still the steaming and the bubbling and the hacking, the grease and the stink, the clatter of chains and the shouting of foremen, the dark hulks of the whales on their slipways beneath the bush, that I would have found here 150 years ago'.

From **Mosman Wharf**, take a short cut through the labyrinth of Mosman's suburbia. At the top of the stairs behind the wharf, take the concrete path on the right, following it up the steep hill of Trumfield Lane. At the top, take the stairs on the right and cross the street to the marked 'Pathway to Raglan Street' directly opposite. Turn right into Curraghbeena Road, and follow it to the end, where there is a playground (Curraghbeena Park). From here, take the curving roadway down through bushland towards the next bay: **Little Sirius Cove**. The rest of the walk is very easy to follow by simply sticking to the shoreline.

Little Sirius Cove **53**

Take the stairs that lead down and around the cliff line. The walk becomes a track and then a driveway, before heading down more stairs to **Sirius Cove Reserve**. Named after *HMS Sirius*, one of the ships of the First Fleet, this is where British warships were overhauled in the early days of the colony; the site was chosen for its remoteness, so mariners wouldn't fall into the wicked bars and brothels of the Rocks.

Today, the Reserve has a playground and tidal swimming pool popular with families on weekends. On the far side of the beach, follow the grassy headland around through a grove of paperbark trees; continue around the shoreline through unspoilt bushland, to the mouth of the bay. This path is a popular jogging trail for local residents, who beam at hikers with the untroubled expressions bred by large amounts of inherited wealth. Over a century ago, artists of the Heidelberg School – such as Tom Roberts and Arthur Streeton – set up the famous Artists Camp along this stretch of shoreline.

As you near the final headland, the path forks off to the right, emerging onto a little rocky viewpoint. Take this short detour to observe a totally different view of the harbour. The undeveloped expanse of Cremorne Point blocks off most of the modern cityscape – presenting a good idea of how this waterline might have looked to the Eora before white settlement.

Back on the trail, take the stone steps down to tiny **Whiting Beach**, one of the most secluded in the harbour and a good spot for a last dip.

From here, it's only a few minutes walk around the shoreline to ★★ **Taronga Zoo** (daily 9am–4.30pm), situated in Athol Bay. After all the peace and seclusion of the walk from Cremorne, arriving at the docks here can be a bit of a shock: on weekends and holidays, you'll be greeted by throngs of other zoo visitors arriving by ferry from Circular Quay. The zoo itself is actually located up a steep hillside. There are two ways of entering: either by catching a bus (waiting by the wharf) up to the main entrance; or by taking the 'aerial safari' ride to the top. If the lines aren't already too long, this latter option is the most exciting: it glides you over the many animal enclosures, and gives you an easy walk back downhill through the zoo.

Whichever way you enter, this is one of Sydney's grandest attractions. Surrounded by virgin bush, it must be one of the most beautiful zoo sites on earth (Taronga is an Aboriginal word for 'water view'). There are more than 5,000 animals in the collection, including the full panoply of Antipodean critters, which are often all but impossible to see in the wild.

Taronga Zoo: koala and admirers

Special attention has been placed on creating natural-looking enclosures, with many of the animals separated from the public by moats rather than fences. The Koala House is like a theatre-in-the-round. A circular pedestrian ramp surrounds a collection of tree trunks upon which hang a number of ever-drowsy koalas (there's not a lot of leaf coverage, so not much opportunity for hiding). Taronga is also your best chance for seeing a platypus: darkened indoor tanks periodically reveal this industrious character, with its distinctive snout, in a relatively natural environment. There's a walk-through environment for kangaroos, and a more solid barrier separating visitors from creatures they might prefer not to encounter in the wild: salt-water crocodiles (the world's largest reptiles) and snakes (Australia has the world's seven most poisonous snakes, as well as 10 of the next 13 – most are several hundred times more toxic than cobras and rattlesnakes). Dingoes (notorious for stealing Azaria Chamberlaine's baby in an Alice Springs campground some years back, provoking Australia's most sensational modern trial and the 1988 Meryl Streep movie *A Cry in the Dark*) seem utterly at home in their vast enclosure.

Reptile ride

The zoo houses plenty of non-Australian animals, if you're interested (the elephants housed on the headland are said to own the best chunk of real estate in Sydney). There are many popular eateries, and if you visit in summer, you might catch one of the classical concerts now being held in Taronga Park's gardens.

From the bottom of the zoo, ferries depart for Circular Quay every 30 minutes.

Route 8

Aboard the Manly Ferry

Seaside and seclusion

Manly Ferry – The Corso – Shelley Beach – North Head – Collins Beach – East Esplanade (4.8km/3 miles)

55

The most famous ferry ride of all is to **Manly**. In fact, this was Sydney's first water service: before the first steam ferry in 1848, the journey from the city could take days, creating endless problems getting supplies to the 12 or so families that lived here in a sleepy fishing hamlet. The introduction of regular transport instantly tied Manly to the port, and encouraged other ferry services to grow. Still, few people bothered with its remote shores until 1857, when a rich emigrant from England named Henry Gilbert Smith realised Manly's potential as Australia's answer to Brighton (he even wanted to change the name to Brighton, but local patriots drew the line).

The combination of harbour ferry ride and seaside views proved irresistible. By the 1930s, Manly was Australia's family holiday resort *par excellence* – a legendary refuge 'seven miles from Sydney and a thousand miles from care'. Today, the basic elements of Manly's lure have not changed. It's still very much a family-style attraction – although recent developments, including some excellent little cafés, have seen a resurgence of interest from a younger crowd.

Fishing in the harbour

Pick up the Manly ferry at Circular Quay for the 30-minute ride. There's also a faster, more expensive JetCat service to Manly, but you can't beat the pleasures of the older boats, where passengers can sit outside and feel the sea breeze on their faces. This is still the cheapest and best cruise in Sydney: running the whole length of the harbour east from the city, the route even crosses through virtually open sea between the Heads. On a rough day, when the waves dwarf other boats, the ferry can be quite a wild ride (if you're prone to motion sickness, this is the time when a JetCat might be the wise choice).

Manly Cove

The ferry slows into calm **Manly Cove**, on the Harbour side of the Manly promontory. (The name was given by Captain Arthur Phillip of the First Fleet, who was speared in the arm by an Aboriginal nearby in 1788; he forbade the usual bloody retaliation, as he found the natives here 'manly'.) Note that the tepid waters of Manly Cove are not the Manly Beach of legend: a century ago, Sir Arthur Conan Doyle came here to visit the famous site, took one look at the cove and returned in disappointment to the city, never getting off the ferry. Manly Beach, of course, is on the ocean side of the isthmus.

Manly amusement park

On alighting, the Coney Island-like quality of Manly today becomes apparent. The garish **amusement park**, rollercoaster, sideshow attractions and fast food stalls that have met visitors for generations are still there on the arrival pier – now supplemented by a massive new shopping mall. To the left of the pier, Manly Cove beach is still a less-than-inspiring sight, although its gradual depth is ideal for toddler swimming. The new attraction here is **Ocean-World**, Sydney's second underwater aquarium (see also Sydney Aquarium in Darling Harbour, in Route 3). It draws big crowds, especially for its shark feeding.

Exit the old arrival pier to the bus stop islands in front. Directly across the street is the beginning of a bustling pedestrian walkway. **Manly Corso** is the main thoroughfare to Manly Beach; on weekends and summer holidays, it can be quite a scene of buskers, tourists, even the occa-

Manly Corso

sional brass band. Although a new contingent of mod-

ern cafés are arriving, the strip is mainly lined with old-style souvenir shops and snack bars – the best and most popular fish'n'chip shops are at the far end of the walkway, near the beach. They can be jam-packed at lunch time, since everyone wants their picnic by the sea. While you wait, check out the facades above the shops: the colourful, sugarbread designs are the essence of 1930s Manly.

From here, you can finally take in the majestic ocean view of ★ **Manly Beach**. A lovely parkway separates the sand from traffic, lined with the towering Norfolk Island pines that Manly's visionary entrepreneur, Henry Gilbert Smith, planted himself back in the late 1850s. Smith's dream of a family-style, Antipodean Brighton may be borne out by Manly's gleeful beach culture today, but it's worth remembering that the area was for decades synonymous with the daring and risqué.

In colonial times, only convicts ocean-bathed – and this was simply in order to wash. When Smith was first promoting Manly, in the middle of the 19th century, swimming was still regarded as sordid: laws restricted bathing to either the early hours of the morning or after dark, when few could be offended by the sight of others in wet, body-hugging outfits. Inspectors patrolled Manly beach by day to enforce these decency laws, and a council official sounded a gong when it was time for swimmers to leave the water.

As the 19th century wore on, the laws became intensely unpopular. Then, in 1902, one William Henry Gocher – editor of the *Manly and North Sydney News* – became the first to openly defy the ban by hitting the Manly surf at midday. Gocher may well have been blind drunk. He simply walked into the water dressed in complete formal attire: frock coat, striped trousers, an umbrella under one arm and a hard hat. Hailed as a local hero, he was never prosecuted. The government quickly admitted the anti-swimming law to be absurd; only five years later, with Manly's waters packed in daylight, Gocher was presented with a gold watch and fifty sovereigns as public thanks for his action.

Take the main beachfront road south (it's called South Steyne), and then the waterfront **Marine Parade** walkway. This is a pleasant meander that continues around the rocky shoreline to **Cabbage Tree Bay**, with its pretty rockpool area known as **Fairy Bower**. There is a tiny, well-loved lunch spot here called **The Bower**, which has great food and fabulous views.

Continue around the walkway to the almost paradisical setting of ★★ **Shelley Beach**. After the bustle and breeze of Manly, everything here seems scaled down in size – from the compact, completely protected swimming bay to

Manly Beach

57

Shelley Beach

the manicured picnic lawn nestled beneath a rich green headland. Shelley Beach's waters are unusually clear and tranquil, making them ideal for snorkeling or scuba-diving (beginners often come here for lessons), while the golden sands provide an ideal showplace for suntanning bods. The original 1920s beachfront kiosk has been turned into a chic restaurant – named **Le Kiosk** – which is always busily serving gourmet Aussie cuisine to some of the best outside tables in Sydney. In slightly off-peak hours, you can pick up coffee and a cake. Afterwards, work off the calories by taking the short climb up the hill; the trail begins directly behind the beach and runs out to the point for fine views of the ocean and rugged coastline.

For stage two of this itinerary, meander back along the Corso to Manly Wharf. From the bus depot in front, take Bus 135 to Manly Hospital; it departs approximately once an hour from Bus Stop 4 (there's also a sign 'North Head Tours' in the bus window). The driver takes you along suburban Manly backstreets, which are dominated by the palatial Victorian sandstone form of **St Patrick's Seminary**, built in 1885. The route then runs into Sydney Harbour National Park, to the edge of ★★ **North Head**.

North Head

At the last stop begins a short walking loop via a lookout point on the very precipice of Sydney Harbour's most dramatic entrance. This circuit – called **Fairfax Walking Track**, after the Fairfax press magnates who own the *Sydney Morning Herald* – passes through Sydney's unique coastal flora. This dry, scrubby, windblown bush is notoriously resilient; devastated by fire a few years back, most of it has successfully regenerated. The circuit takes almost exactly 12 minutes, if you stroll very slowly – at least according to the bus drivers, who have timed the walk and leave after 15 minutes! The viewpoint is located midway along the loop, and provides what is probably the most spectacular view in Sydney (more dramatic than the view from South Head, which is above Watson's Bay and was covered in Route 6). The harbour is usually dotted with sailing yachts, and you can recognise many of the stopovers from earlier routes.

Back on the bus, the driver will drop you at the old **Quarantine Station** if you have made prior arrangement to take a guided visit (tel: 9977 6522). This was the first home for many early immigrants to Australia: it was constructed to protect Sydney from epidemic diseases such as Spanish influenza, smallpox and bubonic plague. Tours pass through a maze of historic buildings including the hospital, disinfecting showers and a mortuary. There are also 'ghost tours' scheduled four nights a week.

Otherwise, ask the driver to let you off at the start of **Collins Beach Road**. Running through the unspoilt bush-

SLOW WILDLIFE CROSSING

Take care on Collins Beach Road

land of the Sydney Harbour National Park, this old down-hill roadway sees virtually no car traffic – with its paper-bark eucalyptus and chattering birdlife, this is about as close to a wilderness walk you can find in any city on earth.

At the road's end, take the track on your right. It will cross two footbridges on its way down to secluded **Collins Beach**. After the second bridge, a stone cairn marks the spot where Governor Arthur Phillip was speared in 1788 by a local Aboriginal named Wil-ee-ma-rin as a result of an apparent misunderstanding. These days, Collins Beach is one of the most secluded and serene little swimming beaches in Sydney. Complete with a peaceful waterfall, this spot is a reminder of how the whole harbour's shore-line must have looked before colonisation. On weekends, the bay fills up with splendid yachts.

Leave the beach via the cliff stairs at the far end of the sand and follow the steep hillside track up to a concrete pathway. Cross Stuart Street and enter **Little Manly Point Reserve**, taking the left fork down to the point itself. This is a popular spot for harbour fishermen who never seem to mind spending a whole day without a nibble. Keep following the path around through the reserve to the next beach, **Little Manly Cove**, favoured by local resident fam-ilies who cluster onto one small crescent of sand. For a final panorama of the city – especially impressive if it's sunset – turn left down Addison Road to **Manly Point Peace Park**.

Stuart Street will take you back to the **East Esplanade** of Manly Cove. Take the low path along the waterfront, where the homely nautical atmosphere of old Manly re-turns with its ageing boatsheds, yacht clubs and amuse-ment pier. You're now back at the wharf, where you can hop on a ferry back to the city.

Collins Beach views

Architecture

Opposite: a Paddington facade

Very little remains of Sydney's earliest colonial architecture, which was constructed by convicts from mud, crushed shell mortar, reeds and unseasoned wood. Even so, the Rocks district bears the scars of the early days: the streets and laneways cut by chain-gangs deep into the sandstone landmass still dominate the street plan, and remain as evidence of early hardship. Other examples of the first convict-era colonial houses are Cadman's Cottage (*see page 24*) and Elizabeth Farm in Parramatta.

The next wave of Australia's early architecture was built in more classic Georgian style. Fine public buildings were designed by former convict Francis Greenway; they can be found particularly along Macquarie Street, which was named after the civic-minded governor responsible for Sydney's transition from a crude penal colony into a small city (*see page 28*). Excellent examples of the private opulence of the early free settlers can be seen in Elizabeth Bay House and Vaucluse House (*see pages 47–48*).

The Victorian era saw a boom in urban development. Sudden wealth of the 1850s gold rush provided for the first 'tall' buildings and grand churches, such as St Mary's Cathedral, the largest in the British Empire. Commercial grandeur arrived in the form of elaborate shopping arcades such as The Strand, and the Romanesque-inspired Queen Victoria Building (*see page 30*).

But the most typically 'Sydney' architectural style, favoured from the 1870s onwards, is the humble terrace house. Thrown up for industrial workers, these quaint, iron-laced dwellings line the narrow streets of whole inner city suburbs like Potts Point, Balmain, Paddington and Glebe. By the 1960s, many were deserted, but artists and writers began moving into them. The relentless process of gentrification began, and today terraced houses are amongst the most expensive slices of Sydney real estate.

Throughout the 20th century, Sydney's CBD (Central Business District) has pursued what can be kindly described as 'an eclectic visual course', with many architectural styles thrown together without much overall design consideration. 'Modern expressionism' has given rise to everything from skyline atrocities like Centrepoint Tower to a score of uninteresting hotel and office towers, as well as more successful experiments – such as Australia Square (which is round) and the country's most famous and visionary building, the Sydney Opera House.

Today's new vogue, 'contemporary expressionism', emphasises structurally designed exteriors, curving silhouettes, rustic Australian motifs and plenty of glass. It can be seen in giant sports stadiums and museums such as the Powerhouse, and the Maritime Museum.

Macquarie Street

61

The Queen Victoria Building

One of the finest views in the world

Performing Arts

The best source for information on the performing arts is the 'Metro' guide in Friday's edition of the *Sydney Morning Herald* (it will also provide the best telephone numbers for booking shows). Most theatres sell tickets through their own box offices, but two main ticket agencies **Ticketek** (9266 4800) and **Firstcall** (9320 9000) sell tickets for major entertainment events. The **Halftix** booth in Martin Place is worth visiting if you're flexible about which show you want to see; it offers half-price tickets to several theatres on the day of the performance.

Walking tall

Theatre and opera

The **Sydney Opera House** is a focal point of fine performance – including classical concerts, opera, ballet, theatre and films – and a night at one of its stages, sipping champagne above the harbour during the interval, is an unforgettable, if pricey, treat. Still, the Opera House certainly isn't the only venue. **The Sydney Theatre Company** has its own spectacular harbourside home in the Wharf Theatre – a renovated old finger wharf in the Rocks – and presents an extensive schedule of productions. This well-appointed and stylish complex, which includes a fine 'New Australian' restaurant, provides a complete night out. The **Sydney Dance Company** is also located here.

Other Sydney institutions are the **Belvoir Street Theatre** in Surrey Hills and the **Seymour Centre** in Newtown, which both have several stages presenting high-quality new and traditional theatre. Well-established smaller venues are the **Stables Theatre** in Darlinghurst, which specialises in Australian playwrights, the **New Theatre** in Newtown, the **Ensemble Theatre** in Milson's Point and the **Footbridge Theatre** at Sydney University. The **Bell**

Shakespeare Company presents the bard in an entertaining and accessible way, while outdoor performances of Shakespeare have become a tradition in summer – *Shakespeare by the Sea* at Balmoral beach and *A Midsummer Night's Dream* in the Botanic Gardens are both classic Sydney experiences.

In fact, during the summer months, Sydney fills up with outdoor concerts. Keep an eye out in the *Herald*'s Metro section for the annual operas in the **Domain**, held on Sunday afternoons. On Friday evenings, there are classical concerts in **Taronga Park Zoo**. The National Parks and Wildlife Sevice has even started concerts on **Sydney Harbour's islands**, Goat, Clarke, Shark and Fort Denison. For a modest sum you can pack a picnic and catch special evening ferries out to these rarely-visited outposts. Most weekends, musicians also gather at the Opera House forecourt, in Darling Harbour and at the Bondi Pavilion.

Large commercial musicals are shown at the **Theatre Royal**, the **Capitol Theatre**, **Her Majesty's Theatre** and the magnificently restored **State Theatre**.

Standup comedy is found in small pubs, notably the **Harold Park**, the **Bat and Ball**, the **Unicorn** and the **Hopetoun** hotels. Again, consult the Metro listings for the latest events.

Children love the **Flying Fruitfly Circus**, an athletic troupe aged between eight and eighteen who perform at various venues every year. Free marionette performances for children are shown at **The Rocks Puppet Cottage** on weekends and school holiday periods. People of all ages tend to enjoy the antics of Circus Oz, which is well worth catching if it's in town.

Film

For its size, Sydney has an unusual number of cinemas to choose from. The more commercial films show at multi-screen complexes on George Street near Town Hall, but for art films, go to the **Valhalla Cinema** in Glebe or the **Third Eye Cinema** in Surrey Hills. In Paddington, choose from the **Chauvel**, the **Verona** or **Academy Twin** for unusual foreign and Australian first releases. On the North Shore are **Walker Cinema** and the Art Deco **Orpheum** in Cremorne, where an organist plays the Wurlitzer every day. In the city, the **Rialto Cinema** and the **Dendy** complex show off-beat fare. The majestic **State Theatre** in the centre of the city has been beautifully renovated and is the premier site of the Sydney Film Festival, held in June. Every January in Bondi, the outdoor amphitheatre of the beachfront pavilion hosts the **Flickerfest International Short Film** and **Short Poppies Festivals**, a scene for student and independent film and video makers.

One for the diary

Street-wise stradivari

Calendar of Events

Chinese New Year

January

Sydney Festival & Carnivale (6–26). Sydney's major arts and entertainment festival including theatre, concerts, food stalls, dance and jazz held throughout the city.

Australia Day (26). Commemorates the landing of the First Fleet in 1788. Celebrations include *the Big Day Out* (a rock music concert at the Sydney Showground), the *Ferrython* (when every boating vessel is out on the harbour for a ferry race) and the *Australia Day Concert* (when popular entertainers take over the Domain in the evening).

Chinese New Year Festival (late Jan or early Feb). Chinatown hosts dragon parades and traditional performances.

February

Gays on parade

Sydney Gay & Lesbian Mardi Gras (5 Feb–2 Mar). A month of events; the most famous is the parade held on the last Saturday evening (early March).

Perspecta (Feb/Mar). Contemporary arts festival held in odd-numbered years, hosted by Art Gallery of NSW.

Bondi Beach Cole Classic (first Sunday). A challenging 2-km (1½ mile) ocean race for all ages.

March

Kings Cross Bed Race (Sunday in mid-month). Fundraising event involves creative 'beds' being pushed through an obstacle course.

Dragon Boat Races (weekend mid-month). Spectacle of decorated boats racing on Darling Harbour's Cockle Bay.

Royal Easter Show (12 days beginning one week before Good Friday). Sydney's agricultural show and amusement park extravaganza, luring farmers and cityfolk.

April

Archibald, Wynne, Sulman and Dobell Exhibitions (on display for six weeks mid-autumn). Australia's most prestigious fine art competitions, hosted by the Gallery of NSW; the winner of the Archibald, for portraiture, is always controversial.

Anzac Day (25 April). Australia-wide commemoration for World War I veterans includes dawn memorial service and march; fervently celebrated in the pubs of the Rocks.

May

Australian Antique Dealers Fair (first weekend). Held at Sydney Showground.

June and July

A Taste of Manly (first weekend in June). Food and wine festival held at Manly Beach.

Bandemonium (mid-June to mid-July). Darling Harbour presents ongoing musical performances of jazz, blues, country and world music.

Sydney Film Festival (two weeks in mid-June). The State Theatre showcases the best of the world's new films.

Biennale of Sydney (held in even-numbered years). International visual arts festival lasting for two months.

August

City to Surf Marathon (second Sunday). The Sydney streets turn into a 14-km (9-mile) course for this marathon event, attracting both international and amateur runners.

A marathon event

September

David Jones Spring Flower Show (first two weeks). The ground floor of Sydney's major department store is festooned with fresh flowers.

Festival of the Winds (second Sunday). The sky above Bondi Beach is filled with kites of all shapes and sizes.

Royal Botanic Gardens Spring Festival (late Sep). The gardens are ablaze with Spring flowers; celebrations include music and dance performances, and food stalls.

65

Aurora New World Festival (late Sep–early Oct). Darling Harbour hosts multi-cultural celebrations, ending in October with the 'Blessing of the Fleet', a Greek and Italian tradition.

October

Manly Jazz Festival (Labour Day weekend). A number of venues in Manly present international and national jazz artists.

Manly jazz

Teddy Bears' Picnic (Sunday late in October). Fund-raising for the Children's Hospital involves fun activities and competitions for kids.

November

Melbourne Cup (first Tuesday). Everyone in Australia stops to watch this famous horse race; one of the few times of the year anyone in Sydney pays attention to Melbourne.

Kings Cross Carnival (first Sunday). Darlinghurst Road hosts a street fair.

December

Carols in The Domain (Saturday before Christmas). Popular family event as carols are sung by candlelight in large open grassland.

New Year's Eve fireworks

Sydney to Hobart Yacht Race (26–31 Dec). Famous blue-water race has a spectacular start in Sydney Harbour.

New Year's Eve (31 Dec). Fabulous fireworks display over Sydney Harbour and much public merriment throughout the city; the Rocks and Opera House area are packed.

Food and Drink

The words 'Australian cuisine' used to evoke gruesome images of meat pies, greasy fish'n'chips and other British horrors. But thanks to mass immigration from the Mediterranean and Asia, as well as a steady supply of premium ingredients, Sydney is today one of the world's most exciting cities for dining out. Throughout the 1990s, there has been a constant boom in 'Modern Australian' cuisine – which mixes styles from every corner of the world, with local specialities – and a growing interest in native foods or 'bush tucker', using Aboriginal secrets.

Although great restaurants are located all over Sydney, there are a number of neighbourhoods or streets that have become most popular. In the city centre, the Rocks has a wealth of seafood restaurants, good pubs and pleasant cafés. Macleay Street in Potts Point is a bustling scene of Modern Australian bistros; Victoria Street from Kings Cross to Darlinghurst is scattered with fashionable cafés. A stroll along Oxford Street in Darlinghurst and Paddington, Glebe Point Road in Glebe, King Street in Newtown, or Campbell Parade in Bondi Beach will turn up one pleasant, reasonably priced bistro after another.

67

For seafood, a visit to the **Sydney Fish Market** in Pyrmont is quite an experience. You can select anything from oysters to blue-eyed cod, have it cooked up to your taste, and then relax outside with a bottle of Chardonnay.

The Fish Market

Restaurant selection

This selection is listed according to the following price categories: $$$ = expensive; $$ = moderate; $ = inexpensive. One crucial note: 'BYO' stands for Bring Your Own (wine) – a custom which allows you to choose from the many economical vintages the country now produces, while keeping costs down. But many of the restaurants are 'licensed' (i.e. have wine lists) as well.

Native Australian
Riberries 'Taste Australia', 411 Bourke Street, Darlinghurst, tel: 02 9361 4929. BYO. The showplace for gourmet native foods. French-born chef Jean-Paul Bruneteau has fine-tuned the preparation of difficult-to-prepare ingredients, presenting dishes like 'chargrilled kangaroo fillet with Tasmanian pepperberries'. $$

Modern Australian
Rockpool, 107 George Street, The Rocks, tel: 9252 1888. Licensed. The cutting edge of Modern Australian cuisine with Asian/European creations that seem to please everyone – for a price. The formal, glamorous environment is in keeping with the bill. $$$

Italian presence

Bennelong, Sydney Opera House, Bennelong Point, tel: 9250 7578/7548. Licensed. There are two venues to choose from here. The original upstairs restaurant now has a supper club feel, while the downstairs restaurant commands the serious foodies with very pricey main courses. $$-$$$

Merrony's, 2 Albert Street, Circular Quay, tel: 9247 9323. Licensed. Comfortable surroundings and consistently excellent, predominantly French dishes. $$$

Paramount, 73 Macleay Street, Potts Point, tel: 9358 1652. Licensed. One of the many happening venues on Macleay Street, with more feats of multi-cultural cuisine in softly lit surroundings. $$$

Wockpool, 155 Victoria Street, Potts Point, tel: 02 9368 1771. Ever-evolving, consistently excellent Australian tribute to Asian food, particularly Chinese and Thai. Incredible views of the city, too. $$

Chinese variations

Chinese

Golden Century, 393-399 Sussex Street, Sydney, tel: 9212 3901. Licensed and BYO. The best Cantonese preparation of the best Aussie seafood. $

Fu-Manchu, 249 Victoria Street, Darlinghurst, tel: 9360 9424. BYO. A designer noodle bar serving quality Cantonese, Northern Chinese and Malaysian dishes. Great value for variety and authenticity. $

Japanese

Unkai, Level 36, ANA Hotel, 176 Cumberland Street, The Rocks, tel: 9250 6123. Licensed. The best sushi in Sydney, with million-dollar views of the harbour. $$$

Yutaka, 200 Crown Street, East Sydney, tel: 02 9361 3818. Licensed and BYO. A relaxing alternative to many prim Japanese interiors. Reasonable prices and extensive selection have earned it the 'best all-rounder' reputation. $$

Thai

Darley Street Thai, 28-30 Bayswater Road, Kings Cross, tel: 9358 6530. Licensed. Annual visits by Buddhist monks feed the hype surrounding this undisputedly excellent restaurant. Adventurous variations on traditional dishes heralds 'Modern Thai' cuisine. $$

Arun Thai, 13/39 Elizabeth Bay Rd, Elizabeth Bay, tel: 9357 7414. Licensed and BYO. Outdoor dining, where vegetarian choices and a well-priced wine list attract hordes of locals. $$

Indian

Oh! Calcutta!, 251 Victoria Street, Darlinghurst, tel: 9360 3650. BYO. Exciting range of dishes include modern innovations such as the popular Kangaroo Sahk Khada. Excellent tandoori with plenty of vegetarian choices. $$

Note that for dirt-cheap Indian food, a 'Little India' has sprung up on Cleveland Street, around the corner of Bourke Street.

Greek

Cosmos, 185a Bourke Street, East Sydney, tel: 9331 5306. BYO. This is Modern Greek cuisine, but don't think the traditional favourites are gone. The owner/chef cooks with his mother, rejuvenating dishes such as 'moussaka' with aubergine, scallops and taramasalata. **$$$**

Vegetarian

Iku Wholefood Kitchen, 25a Glebe Point Rd, Glebe, tel: 02 9692 8720. BYO. This little counter-style café has provided many years of squeaky fresh organic/bio-dynamic dishes to happy Glebian vegetarians. An outdoor seating area, generous servings at great prices and no smoking, make for a thoroughly healthful experience. **$**

Tables with a View

Al fresco dining

Because of Sydney's gorgeous harbour and surrounding beaches, there are now some excellent restaurants with harbour or ocean views:

Bather's Pavilion, 4 The Esplanade, Balmoral, tel: 9968 1133. Licensed. Situated at picturesque Balmoral Beach, the original 1920s bather's pavilion is the perfect place for a long lunch. Modern Australian cuisine in a bright, privileged setting. Weekends are always fully booked. **$$$**

Catalina Rose Bay, Lyne Park, off New South Head Rd, Rose Bay (between ferry wharf and seaplane base), tel: 9371 0555. Licensed. This glass-fronted harbourside bistro provides a serious Mod Oz experience – the terrace being the place to be on a fine day. **$$$**

The Pier, 594 New South Head Rd, Rose Bay, tel: 9327 4187. Licensed. Another idyllic location to sample excellent seafood. Oysters shucked on the spot, Queenland reef fish and spectacular views across the bay. **$$$**

Onzain, Second Floor, Bondi Digger's Club, 232 Campbell Parade, Bondi Beach, tel: 9365 0763. Licensed. The perfect end to a day at Bondi Beach, with long sunset views and succulent French bistro fare. **$$$**

Doyles on the Beach

Doyles on the Beach, 11 Marine Parade, Watson's Bay, tel: 02 9337 1350. Licensed. A Sydney institution with great views, but the seafood dishes, although always fresh, are not as interesting as many of the newer harbourside restaurants. Take a water taxi from Circular Quay. **$$$**

Jonah's, 69 Bynya Rd, Palm Beach, tel: 9974 5599. Licensed. Possibly the best ocean view in… the world. Guests can drive here or arrive by seaplane (special lunch packages include transfers up the mountain) to spend a glorious afternoon with a French Mediterranean feel. **$$$**

Shopping

Window dressing

Sydney's main shopping district is in the heart of the city, in the area bounded by Martin Place, George, Park and Elizabeth streets. Here you'll find large department stores like **David Jones** and **Grace Brothers**, the elegant **Strand** and **Picadilly Arcades**, and the multi-level shopping complexes such as **Centrepoint** (in the base of the tower) that runs between Pitt and Castlereagh streets. The more upmarket **MLC Centre** and **Chifley Plaza** house the international designers such as Gucci, Tiffany and Cartier.

Bargains for overseas visitors include opals and sheepskin products. These items are found in souvenir shops, many of which are located in the Rocks area, as well as the elegantly restored **Queen Victoria Building** on George Street and the newly developed Darling Harbour complex.

A walk along Oxford Street in Darlinghurst and Paddington will take you past endless cutting edge boutiques, both gay and straight fashions, cafés, and cool scenes. At the Paddington end of Oxford Street, a visit to **Paddington Market** (on a Saturday afternoon) is a must: it's located in the churchyard at the corner of Oxford and Newcombe streets, has bargains on jewellery, handicrafts and clothes by young Sydney designers, and provides the best people-watching in Sydney. The backstreets of Paddington are the home of Sydney's fine art galleries, while neighbouring Woollahra (Queen Street) is the established home of antique and rare book shops.

Paddington Market

Another happening market is in Bondi, at the Public School grounds on Campbell Parade, held on Saturday mornings. This has become known for funky 1970s wear which is snapped up early for the night's cavorting.

Australiana
Weiss Art, 85 George Street, The Rocks.
Australian Craftworks, 127 George Street, The Rocks.
Makers Mark, Chifley Plaza, Sydney.

Opals
The Rocks Opal Mine, Clocktower Square, 35 Harrington Street, The Rocks.
Flame Opals, 119 George Street, The Rocks.
Gemstone Boutique, 388 George Street, Sydney.

Aboriginal Art
Aboriginal and Tribal Art Centre, 117 George Street, The Rocks.
Hogarth Galleries Aboriginal Art, 7 Walker Lane, Paddington.
Coo-ee Aboriginal Art Gallery, 98 Oxford Sreet, Paddington.

Nightlife

Drinking in Darlinghurst

Whatever your taste in nightlife may be, it can be satisfied in Sydney. The best guide is the *Sydney Morning Herald*'s Metro section, out every Friday.

A few nightclubs remain fashionable within a sea of ever-changing hip scenes. Most are located in the adjacent suburbs of Darlinghurst, Potts Point, Surrey Hills and Paddington. Oxford Street in Darlinghurst has a number of dance clubs such as **DCM** and **Q**. Just off Oxford Street, the ex-funeral home of **Kinselas** is an interesting venue with a range of gay and straight evenings, as is the **Bentley Bar** in nearby Surrey Hills. While the main street of Kings Cross appears to thrive with all manner of seedy nightlife, the more fashionable dance clubs such as the **Cauldron**, **Sugareef** and the **Tunnel** are located on the backstreets. Fans of '70s music should head for the **Tender Trap** held on Sunday nights at the **VIP Club** in Kings Cross (polyester clothing only).

A night on the town

Big name bands perform at the vast **Sydney Entertainment Centre** and the **Sydney Cricket Ground**. Smaller venues that still feature well known acts are the **State Theatre**, the **Enmore Theatre**, **Metro** and **Selina's** in the Coogee Bay Hotel. The live band scene, however, is most vibrant in the hundreds of pubs that are scattered throughout the city; almost every little place will have live music on Friday and Saturday nights. Some of the best pub venues for live bands are the **Sandringham Hotel**, the **Annandale Hotel** and the **Bridge Hotel**.

Refreshments at hand

For jazz fans, the **Basement** is Sydney's best-loved venue, showing a broad range of international and local performers. The **Strawberry Hills Hotel** has consistently good contemporary jazz. Other ongoing venues are the **Harbourside Brasserie**, the **Orient Hotel**, **Soup Plus** and **Café de Lane**.

Getting There

Opposite: arriving in style

By air

Sydney is Australia's major international airport, with daily flights of more than 25 international airlines arriving from Asia, Europe and North America.

Qantas is the national Australian airline, and usually offers the best deals to Australia. Tickets can be purchased through travel agents, or direct (in the US, the toll-free number is 1 800 227 4500; in the UK, the number is 0345 747 767). Special domestic fares on Qantas are available for international visitors, so you should also purchase your local flights when you buy your ticket to Australia. Ask about the 'Boomerang Pass'.

Australia's two national domestic airlines are Qantas and Ansett Australia. Both operate regular scheduled flights from all locations throughout Australia to Sydney. Again, special offers are usually available.

Qantas reservations: Domestic, tel: 131313; International, tel: 9957 0111.

Ansett reservations: Domestic, tel: 131300.

From the airport, the green and yellow Airport Express buses depart every 10 minutes for the city; it's a distance of 9km (5½ miles), and the bus makes key stops in the city. $5 one way or $8 return. A taxi from the airport to the city costs approximately $20.

By coach

Sydney is serviced by all the major coach companies (the biggest is Greyhound Pioneer Australia, tel: 132030). Most coaches arrive at the Long Distance Coach Terminal at Central Railway Station, Eddy Avenue, tel: 9281 9366.

By train

All interstate and regional trains arrive at Central Station. Australia's principal rail lines follow the east and south coasts, linking Sydney with the major cities of Brisbane, Cairns, Melbourne and Adelaide, (although the famous Indian-Pacific cuts across the vast Nullabor Plain to Perth). The most comprehensive service is operated by Countrylink; reservations are required, tel: 132232.

By car

The major highways into the city are the Princes Highway, which runs along the coast from Melbourne; the Hume Highway, which also comes from the south, although further inland; the Pacific Highway, running along the north coast; and the Great Western Highway, from the west (it turns into Parramatta Road). From any direction, as you approach the outskirts of Sydney, follow the blue and white Metroad signs to the city centre.

73

The Airport Express

Getting Around

The State Transit Authority (STA) operates all public transport in Sydney. There are information and ticket kiosks at the airport, Circular Quay, Wynyard Park and Queen Victoria Building. For information on all STA trains, buses and ferries from 6am–10pm daily, tel: 131500.

A *Sydney Pass* could be a worthwhile investment. It covers all bus and ferry transport, including Sydney Explorer buses, Harbour Cruises, the Tramway (shuttle between Circular Quay and Darling Harbour) and a return fare on the Airport Express. A 3-day *Sydney Pass* is $50; 5 days $65; 7 days $75.

Trains

Electric trains are the quickest way to get around the sprawling suburbs. The CityRail service covers a large area, including the most useful 'City Circle' stations. For CityRail information, Central Station, tel: 9219 4054, or Circular Quay Station, tel: 9224 3553.

Bound for the zoo

Buses

The main bus termini are at Circular Quay, Wynyard and Central Railway Station. The information kiosk is located behind Circular Quay on the corner of Alfred and Loftus streets. A BusTripper ticket allows unlimited travel for one day (prices vary for the area covered), while a Day-Pass can be used on ferries also.

Ferries depart from Circular Quay

Ferries

The green and yellow ferries are by far the nicest way of getting around Sydney. They all depart from Circular Quay, where a Sydney Ferries Information Office (opposite Wharf 4) issues tickets, TravelPasses, timetables and brochures outlining cruise services .

The longest ferry run in the harbour is the trip to Manly, covering 11km (7 miles) in 35 minutes and costing $3.40. For efficiency, the alternative JetCat does the trip in half the time and is slightly more expensive at $5.60. The shortest ferry trips go to Kirribilli and McMahon's Point: both offer stunning panoramas of the city skyline, the Opera House and the Harbour Bridge.

All taxis are metered

Taxis

All Sydney taxis are metered. There is an initial $3 hiring charge (called 'flag fall'), then $1 metered per kilometre thereafter. A phone booking costs $1 extra. The main taxi companies serving the inner city are:

Premier Taxis, tel: 9897 4000; Taxis Combined, tel: 9332 8888, Legion Cabs, tel: 9289 9000; RSL Taxis, tel: 9581 1111.

Facts for the Visitor

A day at the zoo

Tourist information

For brochures and general information overseas travellers should contact the **Australian Tourist Commission**.
In the UK: Gemini House, 10–18 Putney Hill, London SW156AA, tel: 0990 561434.
In the US: 25th floor, 100 Park Avenue, New York, NY 10017, tel: 212-687 6300; Suite 1200, 2121 Avenue of the Stars, Los Angeles, CA 90067, tel: 310-552 1988.
For more specific information there is the Tourist Commission's **Aussie Helpline**. In the US, tel: 800-433 2877; in the UK, tel: 0990 022000.

In Sydney, information and bookings for accommodation and tours is provided by the **NSW Travel Centre**, which has an office in the city centre (19 Castlereagh Street, tel: 9231 4444), as well as a desk at the international airport. The **Sydney Information Booth** often has faster service and is located in nearby Martin Place, tel: 9235 2424. A Tourist Information Service also handles phone enquiries from 8am–6pm daily on tel: 9669 5111.

Cash dispensers and exchange

Automatic cash dispensers are conveniently located throughout the city. Many of these now accept overseas bank cards with the currency being exchanged according to bank rates. Before leaving home, ask your home bank for the address of affiliated services. The leading Australian banks are Westpac, National, Commonwealth and ANZ.

While Australian dollar traveller's cheques are accepted at most stores, foreign currency traveller's cheques can be exchanged at banks, hotels or at the many bureaux de change located throughout the city.

Hotels take traveller's cheques

Sightseeing tours

Sydney Explorer

The red 'Sydney Explorer' bus is an STA tourist service operating a continuous loop around the city's tourist sights. From 9am–7pm daily, it leaves at 20-minute intervals from Circular Quay; a $20 day ticket allows you to hop on and off whenever you like. Covering the Eastern Suburbs coastal route all the way to Watson's Bay, the blue 'Bondi & Bay Explorer' departs every 30 minutes.

The Tramway, a bus that looks like a tram, shuttles between Circular Quay and Darling Harbour every 15 minutes – an all-day ticket costs only $3.

The Monorail circles above the retail centre before crossing to Darling Harbour, its principal function. It costs $2.50 per ride and provides good views.

From Circular Quay, there is a mind-boggling array of Sydney Harbour cruises. Ask locally for details.

Opening times

General retail trading hours for stores are Monday to Friday 9am–5.30pm, and Saturday 9am–4pm. Late night shopping takes place on Thursday until 9pm, although many smaller traders may stay open late on other evenings. Most businesses close Sunday.

Banks are open Monday to Thursday 9.30am–4pm and Friday 9.30am–5pm. Some are open on Saturday mornings. All banks, post offices, government and private offices close on public holidays.

Postal services

For rapid results

Post offices are open Monday to Friday 9am–5pm, although the GPO is open Monday to Friday 8.30am–5.30pm, and Saturday 8.30am–noon. Located at 159 Pitt Street (near Martin Place), tel: 131317.

Emergency

For the police, ambulance or fire brigade, dial 000.

Telephone

Most payphones take cards

Public telephones are located throughout the city – a local call costs 40 cents for unlimited time. Most payphones take phone cards, which can be bought at newsagents and stores in $2, $5, $10, $20 or $50 denominations.

Long distance calls within Australia (STD), are available on most public telephones. STD calls are cheapest after 10pm and before 8am. For International Direct Dial (IDD) calls, dial 0011 followed by country code, city code and number. International public phones may be found at city GPOs, rail termini and airports.

Six-digit telephone numbers commencing with 13 can be called from any public phone in Australia for the price of a local call. Numbers beginning 1-800 are toll-free.

Active pursuits

Thanks to its magnificent harbour and ocean setting, Syd-neysiders are able to enjoy the entire gamut of water-based activities.

The best ocean swimming beaches are Bondi, Manly and Coogee; surfers should head for Tamarama, Maroubra and Narrabeen. Meanwhile, the harbour has its own tiny beaches popular for swimming and sailboarding.

Bondi bathers

Sailing companies such as Sunsail (Lavender Bay) rent out yachts at around $300 a day ($160 extra if you need a skipper). A more economical taste of the harbour can be had for $40: Sunsail runs yachts in the Sydney Harbour races twice a week, and you can come along for the ride. A BBQ dinner, with booze, is even thrown in.

Hiking is a favourite pastime of Australians. Apart from the many ocean and harbour walks available, the Royal National Park (one hour south of the city), is the ideal location for a long wilderness wander. Apart from the walks described in this book, there are a number of hikes closer to the city: pick up the excellent leaflet on the subject 'Go Walkabout with Sydney Ferries', available from the information booths at Circular Quay. Centennial Park in the Eastern Suburbs is a popular choice for cycling, horseback riding and rollerblading:

Centennial Park Cycles, 50 Clovelly Road, Randwick, tel: 9398 5027; Centennial Park Horse Hire and Riding School, RAS Showground, Moore Park; Bondi Boards and Blades, 230 Oxford Street, Bondi Junction or 148 Curlewis Street, Bondi Beach.

Spectator sports

The Sydney Football Stadium is the biggest venue for Rugby League and Rugby Union matches. The Sydney Cricket Ground hosts the international and Test matches. Tickets for both venues are available through Ticketek, tel: 9266 4800.

The yachting season runs from September to May. Hard fought races and regattas are held nearly every weekend between the '18-footers', perhaps the most exciting sailboats in the world. To catch the thrills, a spectator ferry leaves Circular Quay at 2pm. Spectators also turn out in full force each year for the big Sydney-to-Hobart Yacht Race, on 26 December.

Yachting season: regattas are held nearly every weekend

Surfing carnivals are held at one of Sydney's ocean beaches on most Saturdays between October and March. These consist of swimming races, surfboat races and board-paddling events. There are also professional and amateur surfboard-riding competitions in the summer and autumn months, but the location is often not selected till the day of the contest in order to take maximum advantage of the best local surf conditions.

Accommodation

Most of the deluxe hotels are located in the historic Rocks and city area. This has the advantage of being right at Sydney Harbour, but there are other inner city suburbs with harbour views. Fashionable Potts Point, for example, has a wealth of choices, many moderately priced. There's also Bondi, for a beachfront stay, Paddington for the art connoisseur and a host of other attractive locations.

Budget accommodation is mainly found in the Kings Cross area, particularly along Victoria Street, which has a score of private hostels. Budget travellers also head to Bondi Beach or Manly Beach. Bed and Breakfast Sydneyside manages a list of private homes that offer accommodation, tel: 02 9449 4430.

Ritz Carlton-Sydney

International ($$$$ Over $200 per night double)

Ritz Carlton-Sydney, 93 Macquarie Street, Sydney, tel: 02 9252 4600. Classical French furnishings and beautiful paintings create a distinguished ambience. Located close to the Opera House, this is a 'clubby' place, very popular with business people. Excellent restaurant.

Park Hyatt Sydney, 7 Hickson Road, The Rocks, tel: 02 9241 1234. Rated as the most luxurious hotel in Sydney. Spacious, supremely comfortable rooms have privileged water-level views of the harbour and Opera House.

ANA Hotel Sydney

ANA Hotel Sydney, 176 Cumberland Street, The Rocks, tel: 02 9250 6000. Quintessential harbour views from this award-winning 573-room modern tower hotel.

The Observatory Hotel, 89-113 Kent Street, The Rocks, tel: 02 9256 2222. Discreet alternative to the larger hotels, tucked away behind historic Observatory Hill. No harbour views, but truly sumptuous suites with antique-style furnishings; spa baths and excellent service.

Hotel Inter-Continental, 117 Macquarie Street, tel: 02 9230 0200. Grand historic Treasury Building provides the introduction to a spectacular central skylit courtyard, with the accommodation rising above. Many rooms with classic harbour views. Located within minutes of the harbour.

Quay West Sydney, 98 Gloucester Street, The Rocks, tel: 02 9240 6000. Another of the modern towers that front Sydney Harbour, but this one has self-contained luxury apartments. Also a Roman Bath-style swimming pool.

Sir Stamford Double Bay

Premier ($$$ Over $100 per night double)

Sir Stamford Double Bay, 22 Knox Street, Double Bay, tel: 02 9363 0100. Situated in the wealthy suburb, the hotel has fastidious interior decoration, with valuable original artworks. Each room has a carefully designed theme.

Harbourside Apartments, 2A Henry Lawson Avenue, McMahons Point, tel: 02 9963 4300. Terrific harbour and

Opera House views from the north shore. Comfortable apartment style accommodation; ferry at the doorstep.

Australian Hotel

Seventeen Elizabeth Bay Road, 17 Elizabeth Bay Road, Elizabeth Bay, tel: 02 9358 8999. Comfortable one bedroom apartments overlooking Rushcutter's Bay. Convenient location for Potts Point, the city and eastern suburbs.

Simpsons of Potts Point, 8 Challis Avenue, Potts Point, tel: 02 9356 2199. Beautifully restored historic house with period decoration. Close to fashionable eateries.

Medina-Paddington, 400 Glenmore Road, Paddington, tel: 02 9361 9000. Serviced townhouses in a quaint leafy suburb, set in tropical gardens.

Hyde Park Plaza, 38 College Street, Sydney, tel: 02 9331 6933. Overlooking Hyde Park. Large apartment-style rooms include kitchen facilities.

Chateau Sydney, 14 Macleay Street, Potts Point, tel: 02 9358 2500. Harbour views with balconies or city views.

Moderate ($$ Over $80 per night double)

Regents Court, 18 Springfield Avenue, Potts Point, tel: 02 9358 1533. Proud of its arts-oriented clientele. Nestled in a peaceful back street of otherwise seedy Kings Cross.

Coogee Bay Hotel, Corner Coogee Bay Road & Arden Street, Coogee, tel: 02 9665 0000. Heritage-style pub opposite Coogee Beach; ocean views from front rooms.

Victoria Court, 122 Victoria Street, Potts Point, tel: 02 9357 3200, toll free 1-800-63.05.05. Historic terrace house in trendy Victoria Street. Quick train or bus to city.

The Manhattan Hotel, 8 Greenknowe Avenue, Elizabeth Bay, tel: 02 9358 1288. Elegant Art Deco building; some rooms with water views and balconies.

The Hotel Bondi, Corner Campbell Parade & Curlewis Street, Bondi Beach, tel: 02 9130 3271. Bondi's landmark historic pub is a bit raucous, so it is worth staying here only if you get a front room with ocean view.

Budget ($ Under $80 per night double)

Kirketon Hotel, 229 Darlinghurst Road, Kings Cross, tel/fax: 02 9360 4333. A well-run budget house in convenient location, with good facilities.

Wattle House, 44 Hereford Street, Glebe, tel: 02 9692 0879. Clean comfortable hostel in leafy student neighborhood of Glebe. Short walk to Glebe Point Road known for cool cafés, bookshops and art cinema.

Hostels ($12–$20 per person)

Lamrock Hostel, 7 Lamrock Avenue, Bondi Beach, tel: 02 9365 0221. Dorm and twin rooms in old-style house.

Jolly Swagman Hostels in Kings Cross, also called Sydney Central Backpackers. Tel: 02 9357 4733; 02 9358 6600; 02 9358 6400. Famous among travellers.

At your service

Index